T0195859

Brighton MOURNING

The **B-RIGHT-ON** Circuit of Bright

Kathleen Stone, Ph.D

BALBOA.PRESS
A DIVISION OF HAY HOUSE

Balboa Press books may be ordered through booksellers or by contacting:

Balboa Press
A Division of Hay House
1663 Liberty Drive
Bloomington, IN 47403
www.balboapress.com
844-682-1282

Because of the dynamic nature of the Internet, any web addresses or links contained in this book may have changed since publication and may no longer be valid. The views expressed in this work are solely those of the author and do not necessarily reflect the views of the publisher, and the publisher hereby disclaims any responsibility for them.

The author of this book does not dispense medical advice or prescribe the use of any technique as a form of treatment for physical, emotional, or medical problems without the advice of a physician, either directly or indirectly. The intent of the author is only to offer information of a general nature to help you in your quest for emotional and spiritual well-being. In the event you use any of the information in this book for yourself, which is your constitutional right, the author and the publisher assume no responsibility for your actions.

Any people depicted in stock imagery provided by Getty Images are models, and such images are being used for illustrative purposes only. Certain stock imagery © Getty Images.

Print information available on the last page.

ISBN: 979-8-7652-3124-1 (sc)
ISBN: 979-8-7652-3126-5 (hc)
ISBN: 979-8-7652-3125-8 (e)

Library of Congress Control Number: 2022913131

Balboa Press rev. date: 09/23/2022

Contents

Dedication

This book is dedicated to my husband, Floyd Stone, lovingly referred to as Pops. We were blessed to have Brighton join our lives as my fulfilled dream of an exquisite English Crème Golden Retriever from the Netherlands. Brighton was equally fond of Doc and Pops. Brighton gracefully gained angel wings in crossing the rainbow bridge, embraced within our forever love. Little did Pops know that Brighton was truly his forever angel and would be waiting all too soon on the other side of the rainbow bridge to be reunited and embraced with forever golden angel love. This heartfelt story is a tribute to both my forever angels who watch over my shoulder as evidence to believe in everlasting life and love.

Acknowledgments

· ·

This book is a personal journey through end of life and afterlife. It is meant to convey the message of everyday angels that support us with the grace as we integrate the profound mystery of death. Plus, there are clues of synchronicity that are experienced through others, and they enhance the belief that the spirit remains with us in afterlife.

Throughout the book, I share the gentle support and love from our son, James. It is seen in his experiences as a little boy with my many bunnies. This evolved over several decades to the comfort in our loss of Brighton, and the profound sudden passing of his beloved Dad. James's wife, Michelle, is a family angel who has truly been "in the wings" and ready to support and understand in so many calm, subtle ways.

Special acknowledgement is extended to Ans Schuurman of the Morning Valley Kennel in the Netherlands. She had the faith and trust to honor me with her precious puppy, Brighton, when I was a total stranger who connected with her in 2006 through email from America. Over the course of Brighton's life, we became friends, and one of the thrills of our life was for Pops and me to visit Ans in 2012 at her exquisite Netherlands location. That same year, we were blessed to have Ans grace us with a second puppy, our Snowdon, from Polar Express of the Morning Valley. Again, after we had lost Brighton, Ans honored our love for the Morning Valley and Brighton's heritage, and graced us with our Enzo, from Slice of Lemon of the Morning Valley.

Another English Crème Golden Retriever breeder became a personal friend who supported me through the years from the time Brighton first arrived in 2006. Nancy Hagan of Heroes Gold in Elmhurst, Illinois, was there for me through many moments of anxiety as to which puppy I would be receiving from the Netherlands. She shared her veterinary staff expertise related to many health issues and provided seasoned breeder guidance related to many golden retriever behaviors. She held my hand through OFA certifications and the sponsoring of Snowdon for stud services through her Heroes Gold website. She supported me through every moment of Brighton's passage and was the first angel I contacted in the middle of the night when he passed.

There are no words to fully express the appreciation I have for Burr Ridge Veterinary Clinic. All the staff demonstrated such love for Brighton. Dr. Brian Rooney was Brighton's hero when, as a seven-month-old pup, Brighton's ingesting of towel threads led to the need for a lifesaving removal of eighteen inches of intestine. At age six, Brighton again was blessed with the canine cancer expertise of Dr. Jeffrey Palmer, who surgically removed a mast cell tumor with safe margins that did not need further treatment and gave Brighton a full life to the age of thirteen. It was Dr. Palmer who also showed such understanding and compassion toward me as I struggled with the end-of-life decisions that resulted from Brighton's spleen tumor diagnosis that is covered in this book. I have the greatest admiration for all veterinarians, and that also includes Dr. Jacqueline Vernot, animal eye specialist, and Dr. Steven Abel, surgeon, from VCA Aurora Animal Hospital. Likewise, what is truly remarkable is the canine cancer vaccine research of Dr. Mark J. Mamula, of Yale School of Medicine.

When Brighton was in the waning months of his life, another angel appeared to guide us through the phase of hospice and readiness for passage. Dr. Melissa Trupia provided heroic support through her in-depth at-home end-of-life assessment, plus counseling as to the steps to expect in the gradual tumor growth and eventual time of passage. Dr. Melissa has the exceptional gift of being able to provide at-home acupuncture, and her frequent visits were a grace for Brighton, as well as for Pops, Snowdon, and me. She coached me in emergency readiness, plus prescribed and trained me in the use of a syringe with a tranquilizer and pain relief that became a blessing at the end of Brighton's life. Dr. Melissa's at-home practice specializes in hospice care and euthanasia when the time is right. I can't say enough about how such at-home care and euthanasia contributes to the reverence for our fur angels and their dignity in end-of-life care. That level of deep respect is also extended to the professional manner displayed by the Hinsdale Pet Cemetery in honoring final arrangements.

I have profound appreciation for the personal friends who have also lost their fur angels and supported me through their own end-of-life experiences, which are shared in the book through the legacy of their angel dogs: Dr. Angie Bartolomei-Balodimas (Aries, Rocco), Dr. Steve and Sandy Ruby (Benson, Princess, Katie), Ruth Green (Daytona, Jackson), Mamie Kiyohara (Clumber Spaniel), Darlene Salerno (Max), and Bob Wimmi (Shilo). Dog-lover friends from my school district knew Brighton, and we shared love and compassion as we experienced mutual grief in the loss of our fur angels: Pam Dlhy (Hershey), Sandy Morgan (Emma, Abby), and Mary Beth Niziol (Missy, Louise).

Finally, this story of fur angel love and loss could not be complete without the meaningful friendships on Facebook through multiple dog-related groups for golden retrievers and breeders, canine cancer, and pet loss: Laurianne Bagarre (Owen); Julianne Corbin, PhD (Cecelia, Bridgit); Tony Corrigan (Paddy); Robin Falco (Emily Snow, Noah); Debbie Franklin (Theo); Sharon Griggs (Max); Kathleen Herman (Kayleigh); Alice Rocque-Angemeier (Cobe, Callie Rose); Sarah Van Drunen (Chief); and Basia Wilder (Harley).

My sincere thanks to Tricia Montgomery, founder of K9-Fit Club, who knew Brighton and continues to support me in all my dog endeavors. Russell Helms also provided extensive editing and input in the initial manuscript. Lt. Col. Ned Matich (retired) gave me valuable technical assistance in connection with the images used in the book, and thanks to Brent Ohlmann for intellectual property advice.

The staff at Balboa Press has provided excellent support in all phases of the publishing of the book. I feel honored to have the book published by Balboa as a division of Hay House Publishing Company and the inspirational legacy of Louise Hay.

No book on pet loss would be complete without acknowledging all the published authors who have written books about pet loss and the afterlife, including recognized pet communicators. I have provided a list of the resources that I reviewed in helping me to cope with my personal loss, as well as to increase my own depth of integration of the gift of pet communication. The death of pets leads to greater grief and anguish than many realize, and pet death is very difficult for many to even discuss or view in movies. These authors are truly blessed with grace and courage to invest their gifts of spiritual insight and writing in these profound resources that help to comfort others who suffer heartbreaking pet loss.

This is a memoir that integrates deep grief with spiritual faith. I have been blessed through the wisdom of Alan Weintraub. Plus I recognize inspiration gained in the Enneagram webinars of Robert Holden and Caroline Myss. Finally, the webinar guidance of David Kessler of grief.com has supported and guided me to subsequent certification as a grief educator.

1

··

Dry Eyes

My name is Doc. I have a simple story to share of a young girl whose life evolved along the path of love for an angel golden retriever named Brighton.

There is a special photo of me as a little girl of four. I am standing beside my mixed-breed large dog that was light brown with white areas, including a patch on its back hip that looked like a chicken. This female dog of my childhood was named Skip, but as a toddler I had called her Dee, and everyone came to know our family dog as Dee. She was part of our family for many years, and I recall the number thirteen or fourteen to mean that a dog had attained the age of being very old and graced with bonus years in life. As a schoolgirl, I got involved in the outside life of a typical kid and would return home from school to say hi to Dee. My Dad was a milkman and left in the wee hours of morning to deliver milk and return home in early afternoon. It was the standard during my childhood for my mom be a traditional homemaker.

One day in second grade, I came home from school and found that Dee was gone. I looked everywhere but couldn't find her, so I asked my mom. "Mom, where is Dee?" I was in our big old kitchen, in my school dress and standing pigeon-toed in my brown-and-white saddle shoes.

My tall, mustached dad was leaning on the back porch doorway, with his eyes looking downward toward mom. She was standing stiff and tall with her hands in her apron pockets.

"Well, Kathy, you know that Dee had been getting old and has been sick," said Mom.

"Yeah, but where is she?" I could feel tears pushing behind my eyes.

My dad slipped into the kitchen chair to be closer to me and tried to have his tired eyes meet mine. "Dee was sicker than we knew, and she's not coming home. I'm sorry."

I suddenly felt numb and didn't know what to say.

My usually always-poised mom spoke while twisting a dish towel. "Just think of her taking a long sleep where she's not in any more pain."

I figured that this sudden disappearance was the way with dogs, but I was still stunned and feeling very sad.

Protecting me as an innocent little girl, my parents had given me a short, simple explanation that Dee had been sick, and they had to take her to the vet. No details were offered, just the sudden realization that somehow Dee had been "put to sleep" and would never be coming back. It was a simple, almost unexplainable exit, with little emotion and commotion. It became the mysterious end that just happened to dogs.

When I was a teen, we again had a family dog, a beautiful German shepherd named King. He was living in our home when I was married, and his aging process happened after I moved out of the house. So, without my parents' effort to share, I was not made aware when he passed. King also one day became part of the quiet, unspoken "going to sleep" mystery.

At that time, I had been married and was attending college, plus we had a little boy who was the center of our life, but I had never lost the lingering love of dogs. As a young married family, however, we could not have a dog. My newlywed husband had asthma and hay fever and was allergic to cats and dogs. Our married life had no room for pets, with an allergy-prone household that became a barrier to any animals.

After our little boy was born, he eventually grew into a school child and began to ask for a dog. My heart went out to my son, who reluctantly accepted the allergy limitations of his dear pops. Yet, through my family experience, I had the seed planted in me as to the value of a dog.

My son still recalls his perspective of having a dog from his experience with a good friend: "A lot of my friends have a dog. I sure wish I could have one as a pal. It would be such fun."

I knew as an only child that my son dreamed a typical young boy's wish for a frisky fur buddy. Yet with my husband's allergies, there was no way Pops or his allergist would change their minds. My son would regularly remind me, "Most of my friends have smaller dogs. You know my best friend has his small black dog named Bear. We play with him all the time. It's great fun when Bear chases and wrestles with us, and we love to play fetch!"

It was not difficult to acknowledge my understanding of our family dog dilemma, yet I'd have to patiently respond. "And you know how Pops complains about Bear being such an obnoxious barker. With Bear living right behind us, Pops hears him bark for hours, begging to be let off the leash or in the house."

My son would nod his head and grumble, "I know that. Bear doesn't make a lot of friends with the neighbors."

Our suburban house with Bear as our noisy neighbor had a huge finished basement. I genuinely empathized with my six-year-old son's growing interest in having a pet. One day, I looked at that basement and suddenly began to develop an "Aha" plan in my problem-solving way. I investigated what small pet we could get and came up with the idea of a bunny, based on some bunnies that my son and I had seen for sale in a local pet store. The bunnies in question were medium-sized. The cute black and white ones were called Dutch rabbits. My idea was a large rabbit cage in a nice wood paneled extra room in the basement that was never used.

My little boy watched me in amazement as I acquired a large wire rabbit cage. It was set on a platform about eighteen inches off the floor, with a little flat deck area that was like a porch for the bunny when the crate door was open. The legs of the cage were set about three inches above the open wire floor of the cage. In that way, any droppings from the bunny would fall through on newspaper, to be easily cleaned up. Likewise, the cage was large enough that a cat litter box could also be placed at one end. The room was off limits to my allergy-prone husband and became the animal haven for my son and me.

My son said, "Gosh, having a bunny is super! What will Pops say?"

I was definitely stretching the boundaries with Pops, but explained, "We'll have the rabbit in its own room in the basement and clean up the hair regularly so none gets outside the bunny room. We'll make it a peaceful setup, so Pops won't even know the bunny is there."

My son and I would take turns changing the litter box. However, school would keep us quite busy, and we frequently would wait too long. My son sometimes recalls, "The litter box really smelled in that room!"

Time would fast forward through the years for our bunnies. A Dutch rabbit named Peter was our first. My son was in third grade at age eight when we got Peter, and he actually won a trophy in the local pet parade for pulling a pedal race car with Peter as the race car driver. The car had the title "Rabbit Transit" on it. It was somewhat comforting for my son to have a real pet to hop around with and to hold, but isolation in the basement had limitations.

I asked my son to recall what it was like to have bunnies as pets. He admitted that he found it tough to emotionally bond with bunnies. "Rabbits are not the most amiable when it comes to holding or affection. When trying to cuddle some of these bunnies in my arms, I would be left with battle scars. They would flop their powerful hind feet, leaving long scratch marks. We learned to always have a towel ready to wrap around their bodies before picking them up. They also seemed to always be nervous when let outside the cage, with their elevated heart rates, breathing, and restlessness on full display. Unfortunately, as they would hop, they would also drop little hard black beads, an unpleasant but natural habit."

By the last of my rabbits, my son was married, living out of state, and age thirty-two. In between were twenty-four years of acquiring new bunnies that would quickly grow into rabbits, live out their natural lifespans, and die what always felt like too soon. Our backyard became our bunny cemetery, and mom and son bonded too many times in the sadness of the burial process.

After our first Dutch rabbit died quite suddenly, I became aware of a larger rabbit about the size of a cat that had long, drooping ears like a dog. This breed was called a lop-eared rabbit, and it became our enhanced bunny adventure. There was a breeder of lop-eared rabbits located in a suburb about thirty minutes from my home. This was strictly a home-based rabbit breeder with a large shed on the property that was the base of the breeding business. She specialized in mini-lop rabbits with medium-length droopy ears. I bought our first mini-lop bunny, and as my son's interests grew in sports, the bunny enchantment began to take over me, his mom.

Mini-lop bunnies are the cutest things on earth! The new bunny took over Peter's cage. Before long, I felt it was a lonely life for a darling bunny by itself. Soon, I created a second bunny condo setup in the bunny room and acquired a second mini-lop rabbit so the two would have company. The first rabbit was named Thumpy, and he was a darling brown and white bunny. The second bunny was Caesar, and he was a regal, medium gray. I became known as the bunny lady to my friends.

With rabbits as pets, I began the initiation into ongoing grief. When you read about acquiring a pet, the number of life years is discussed, but it doesn't quite click as to the heartbreak that the particular lifespan number represents. Rabbits tend to live three to five years, and true to form, the bunnies in our history tended to live about three and a half years. The bunnies had become my pets and my cumulative saga of grief.

What I didn't realize with bunnies is that they can quickly develop a respiratory illness called snuffles that may unexpectedly take their lives in just a few days. I learned to always be on the alert for any little creamy nasal discharge or milky drops in the corners of the eyes. Those symptoms became a red flag and required an immediate appointment with the vet. Not every vet treats rabbits, so I also had to find a vet who had a specialty practice for small animals. Luckily, there was a bird and exotic animal hospital about twenty minutes from my home, and they were amazing. Each time a bunny developed snuffles, there was a rush to the vet for drops and instructions for care. It also meant a careful regime of constant care and worry for days in the effort to combat the potentially deadly illness.

Over a period of twenty years after the first mini-lop rabbit, I had two mini-lop rabbits at a time, and each time they would turn age three, I would start to get nervous that the hourglass of their lifespan was starting to empty. When the rabbits would pass, normally between ages three and four, I would grieve deeply and yearn to replace the rabbit with a new bunny. So, over a period of twenty years, all too often I would experience the sudden death of my treasured mini-lops, the subsequent grief, and then a renewal with the acquisition of a new bunny to start the life cycle all over again.

One day when my son was in seventh grade, he had rushed home from school to find me shocked and in tears. Pops was out of town, so he was the only one there to help.

"Hi, Mom! What's the matter? Why are you crying?"

I had come home ahead of him to find the Thumpy of that time dead in his crate. By myself, I felt stunned and cried, "Oh, no! What will I do?"

My son had arrived home in a hurry, as we were scheduled to leave in an hour to return to school. "Mom, I have the band concert!"

I hurriedly began instructions, as it was fall, and it would be getting dark early. "Go get a shovel, while I wrap up Thumpy. I have a small case to use as a casket."

We both went into overdrive. I prepared a soft towel inside the little cosmetic case and wrapped everything in a final heavy plastic bag. Within twenty minutes, we were digging a large hole in the flower bed along the back of the house. As the darkness of early night set in, the burial was complete, and we stood in repose sharing tears and exhaustion. We then hurriedly ran back in the house, my son dressed in his band uniform, and grabbed some leftovers as a quick supper. We arrived at school just in time for the concert and settled into the stunned aftermath of dealing with a sudden death.

I went through the grief of losing my sweet bunnies too many times. Often, out of self-preservation, rabbits hide their illnesses and then suddenly collapse and die. There were at least four times when I went down to the basement to feed the bunnies and found one dead in its cage. It was a terrible shock each time, leaving me alone in a situation bearing the sole responsibility to carefully wrap the body and decide how to orchestrate the final resting place. There was one year when my husband's mother came over each day to feed the rabbits while we were on vacation, and it was devastating that one died under her watch. I still have the heartbreaking letter from her that was on the kitchen table when we came home from vacation, telling us how the rabbit had just suddenly died, and she had arranged to have it buried in our yard. There were at least four rabbits buried deep in the flower bed along the back of our house.

My son had a more reasonable perspective. "I enjoyed them as pets, especially our first one, but I didn't have the same level of grief as Doc when they died. I was sad, but Doc took their deaths really hard. Doc took on the role of nurse and almost willed her way to 'save' each bunny, only to be disappointed time after time."

Often, circumstances involved extraordinary care needed for a rabbit while we were scheduled for vacation. One rabbit had developed a head tilt almost like a ministroke that limited neck movement, yet not serious enough to warrant euthanasia. So, I found an animal-care lady who boarded and cared for the compromised rabbit in her home while we were gone.

Another year, I had one mini-lop with a serious respiratory issue, and I had to leave the bunny in the care of the vet hospital while we left on a long-planned vacation to Hawaii. I would anxiously check by phone every day, and on the fourth day of a wonderful trip to paradise, I received word from the hospital that my bunny had died, and they offered to keep the body frozen until I returned home.

My son was the best witness to my grief over the years. "Whether it was burying one of our bunnies in the backyard ninety minutes before my band recital, or being an emotional rock for Mom as she grieved the loss from an ocean away, the losses of our bunnies accumulated to take a toll on Doc."

When the first Thumpy passed, the next bunny was again named Thumpy, and there were five Thumpys in my legacy, to the point that Thumpy became my code name. The last Thumpy was acquired from a quality breeder and lasted seven years, with extraordinary measures applied to extend its life. I wrote a beautiful biographical poem to honor the special name of Thumpy.

One day, I asked my son to recall his childhood with the bunnies. He made a humorous retort, "You mean the turnstile of Thumpies?"

I acknowledged, "Yes, there were so many Thumpies over the years. Plus, I put so much time and effort into nursing them during their frequent sagas of illness."

My son shook his head in dismay. "I have vivid memories of the times where you would place a yogurt-and-medicine concoction into a syringe. I would hold a squirming Thumpy tightly in a towel, while you would try to force-feed him like a baby. It was amazing how you would sometimes handle the whole treatment yourself!"

I chuckled and said, "And I remember when you helped me by holding Thumpy still while I would place drops in his eyes after cleaning out built-up crust due to the recurring mucous from the snuffles virus."

My last bunny was diagnosed with cancer, ironically after I had completed months of cancer treatment. This final Thumpy ended up having a sudden death seizure while I was holding her in my arms and screaming for help. Death situations like that are traumatizing, not knowing what to do, as one feels the life suddenly drain out of the body into spirit. That crystalizing experience gave me a profound feeling that life goes somewhere. It reminded me of the often-quoted science premise that energy can neither be created nor destroyed. The life energy had suddenly left the body, yet I sensed it had not just vaporized but rather invisibly traversed elsewhere.

I have followed several Facebook rainbow bridge support groups that you can reach out to for comfort with the loss of dogs and cats. Yet, I can say from my experience that a rabbit has the same level of love experience as a dog or cat. In the course of twenty-four years, I dealt with pet loss grief at least seven times. I took each death as hard as the loss of a cat or dog, yet the deaths were on nature's timeline, without need for euthanasia. By the same token, each loss was quick and unexpected, leaving the sudden shock and guilt of not knowing, and, in one case, actually being there holding the bunny at the time life left the body.

People who are not attached to animals will try to console you by saying, "Oh, it's just a dog or cat, and it can be replaced." The value placed on a pet rabbit, or guinea pig, gerbil, or bird, is even less. Yet, the emotional grief and pain of losing a small pet, like my rabbits, was every bit as profound. Nevertheless, even friends and family who are dog owners would discount the value of losing a rabbit. I tried to minimize my grief by avoiding talk with anyone who would not understand, yet the grief haunted me whenever anyone would say, "How are you?" in a friendly way, not expecting a response that my bunny had died and that I was sad. I noticed each time that there would be a lump in my stomach that would hang on for weeks as a kind of unspoken malaise.

The reality of the loss of all my rabbits and the subsequent grief was haunting. For each one, the only way I could get past the grief was to get another bunny. It would obsess me, and I would begin searching. At first, I went back to the same local homespun breeder. However, the more I learned about snuffles, the more I realized that the simple backyard environment, the lineage of the breeder's stock, and the snuffles transmission within the group could all be factors in limitations of health and lifespan.

With the last few bunnies, I had been so adamant in finding a quality breeder that in a record downpour, I drove two hours with several family members to the Wisconsin State Fair on the one day the rabbit judging was to take place. The whole fair was in a flooded state, but we walked through the deep puddles with plastic bags on our feet until we got to see the top breeder rabbits and found quality breeders to contact about a new bunny.

The absurdity of us going to the Wisconsin State Fair in terrible conditions is summarized by my son: "As Doc struggled to make sense of the limited lifespan of our rabbits, she became convinced it was an issue of breeding and that if we found a better breeder, we would have 'better rabbits.' This tenacity and focus led Doc to drag me and both of my grandmothers across the border into Wisconsin for a two-hour, rain-soaked drive, only to arrive at the fair in absolutely quagmire conditions. Mud, huge puddles, an incessant downpour, and stench only an animal fair can offer made the experience memorable, but my grandmothers and I began to question Doc's thought process! Outwardly, we were all supportive, but internally, we were thinking 'all this for a rabbit?'"

I can look back now somewhat apologetically when I asked my son what he remembers about that outrageous trip in flooded conditions to the state fair. He said, "I recall the incredible patience and understanding my grandmothers had during this trip, never expecting to be taken so far out of their comfort zones in such miserable conditions, yet having pity on Doc, as they could see how much finding that next breeder meant to her. From Doc's perspective, however, the absurdity avoided her. She happily wrapped her feet in plastic bags, found tarps and umbrellas to navigate through the rain without being soaked, and reveled in the animal immersion throughout the fair. Interestingly, we had to walk through almost the whole fair to get to the rabbit section, which my grandmothers and I noted was a tough walk between the heavy rain and moisture, combined with the pungent odors across the various animal pens. Doc's mom commented to me as we trudged along: 'Once she gets an idea in her head, she just goes after it and doesn't let anything stand in her way.' Very true."

The point I want to emphasize is the intensity related to grief. On multiple occasions, the only way I found to get past the death of a bunny was to replace the void in my heart with a new life, a new beginning. I learned that each bunny was different, and I could not exactly replace the bunny that had been lost, but the inspiration of a new life was the healing process for me. That is why when someone loses any pet, I tactfully imply that he or she may need to eventually get another animal as part of not replacing but rather moving beyond with new life and joy.

My son reflects on how much more I needed to replace a bunny that had died. He expresses such wisdom about how my self-worth was tied to how well I can save and heal. "For me, I was sad to see each bunny die and found myself all too often digging graves for bunnies in our backyard, something my friends were not doing. I did not have the same obsession to replace one the way Doc did over the years. Reflecting on why, I think it's due to my more pragmatic and balanced approach to life versus Doc's highly emotional perspective and her mothering approach to healing. Whether with bunnies, kids at school, her dogs later in life, or with Pops, Doc has always been a caretaker, and her worth is tied to how well she can save and heal her patient. She had to learn that, sometimes, no matter what you do, life isn't always in our control."

So, based on the level of my experience with rabbits, I can now transition to my wisdom about *lifespan*. Emotionally, when I first got a rabbit, I was determined that I could beat the odds of the published lifetime. When I lost my first rabbit, I looked at what I had done wrong and was determined to do better the next time. Yet, each time, I developed a gnawing cloud passing over the joy pf my pet's third birthday, realizing that this may be its last year of life.

With the loss of the last Thumpy, I was inspired to write this poem to celebrate Thumpy's life:

Thumpy

A little furry lop-eared bunny,
With delicate droopy chocolate ears,
Silky caramel and white-patched fur,
And a brown nose with a tiny white tip.
Exquisite little white front paws.
And big, white, strong thumpin' rear feet!
Thumpy lived joy in simple delights,
With excited grunts, hops, and turns.
Greeting me every morning,
Waiting for a hug
And stroke of his beautiful fur,
Then diving into his treat of oats,
And voraciously chomping
On his beloved carrots.

Seven is a special number for me,
And for seven years of good fortune,
Thumpy's unconditional love was mine.
The inexplicable bond of best buddy.
My computer password became "Thumpy"!
With my pet … an unspoken synergy,
For Thumpy had the quiet essence of nature,
Strength to attract without making a sound
Eternal youth like a little puppy.
So cute, he'd melt your heart.
To hug Thumpy in my arms,
And delight in his joy
Of crunching carrots and celery.

The years passed in simple pet contentment.
Always perky ... munching his days through life,
Gaining the nickname of "dump truck,"
Few physical inklings of life's passage.
Moving from spring to summer to autumn.
'Til winter suddenly reared its gloomy season.
The sudden malaise of his turned head,
Sadly became Thumpy's finest hour.
We desperately reached out for help
And were touched by the angels of the animals,
Who caressed Thumpy in their healing arms
And loved him too.

The synchrony of the Thumpy connection,
The hospitality of Janice's loving care,
Cyberspace updates in Rome and Paris,
Dr. Mori's gifts of modern medicine,
A weeping eye flushed by Dr. Nye,
And the holistic needles of hope from Dr. Becker.
His final holiday weekend in Michigan,
And his reaching the inevitable,
With the care of his mommy.
I held him, fed him, and was there for him,
Soothing him with the gift of peaceful music,
Comforting his passage from that worn little body
Into a lively eternal energy in our hearts.

Thumpy will always live on
As an image of nature's wonder.
Remembering his twitching nose and droopy ears,
Hearing the sound of his crunching and munching,
Feeling the silkiness of his beautiful rabbit fur.
The profound spirit of life beyond life ...
Thumpy!

From Bunny to Brighton

If I look at my multiple experiences with the lifespan of my rabbits, it also transferred to my decision to get a dog. I had, for one thing, been worn out from grief every three to four years. I knew that if dogs were healthy, they lived ten to fourteen years, and cats even longer. A good friend of ours in Canada had a golden retriever that lived quite well to the age of fifteen and created a hope-filled potential. Lifespans became an important piece of consideration. I had a brother who had been a breeder of St. Bernard dogs, and I had always been shocked when they would lose most of their Saints around the age of eight. Yet, if one looks at the lifespan of very large dogs, one will find that the larger dogs have shorter lifespans, and the smaller dogs have longer lifespans. I knew I would eventually need to deal with the profound passing of the dog. It elicits such intense grief that I frequently hear from others that it is one of the worst experiences in their lives. Many reach the point where they cannot bear to get another dog, as they can't cope with the anguish of loss another time. Others wait a very long time before embarking on the pet journey again.

I had recently completed a year of cancer treatment when my last rabbit died in my arms. In recovery from cancer, a personal "bucket list" becomes a genuine reality. After recovery, I had been on a cable car in Switzerland and became enchanted by an exquisite white dog that stood beside me on the mountain journey. I did not know the breed, but it became a reality on my bucket list to discover that type of breed and then restructure my home environment in such a way as to acquire one of those enchanting white dogs for myself.

After much research and investigation, I learned the angel dog that had gained first place on my bucket list was an English Crème Golden Retriever. In research about the breed, I learned the published lifespan was about eleven to twelve years. That number loomed in my grief-scarred psyche as a reassuring comfort. If the average lifespan was eleven or twelve, then surely with the best of care, I could have my new angel reach the age of thirteen, fourteen, or perhaps older. The number thirteen became a benchmark in my mind, a sign that was beyond the expected lifespan.

When I finally did get my English Crème Golden Retriever as a pup, I had been able to research the complete pedigree of Brighton on the K-9 data website. In clicking on each of the ancestors in Brighton's pedigree line, I discovered that many included the date of birth as well as the year each one crossed the rainbow bridge. In investigating at least a dozen dogs from Brighton's pedigree or breeder, I saw that the average age they lived seemed to be around eleven or twelve, and these were from top breeders. So, the actual data confirmed the published years and gave me a benchmark of expected lifespan for Brighton.

With Brighton's expected age projected as eleven or twelve based on his ancestors, the magic number *thirteen* registered in my mind,. If Brighton were to reach his thirteenth birthday, he would be gliding into the dessert of life beyond expectations. It is almost the way humans feel when a family elder reaches the age of ninety. In fact, the general formula for dogs is one dog year equals seven human years. That would mean eleven dog years would be seventy-seven, twelve dog years would be eighty-four, thirteen dog years would be ninety-one, and fourteen dog years would be ninety-eight human years. Bingo! It is such a comparable parallel between humans living to an extraordinary age of over ninety, and dogs living to the extraordinary age of thirteen or more. It all makes rational sense, but emotionally, it is devastating. Thirteen is beyond an expected lifespan, at least for a medium- or large-size dog!

The more I investigated potential lifespans, the more I also reviewed a book I had acquired several years before. Yet until Brighton's age of eleven, I had not closely reviewed the guidelines related to an aging dog.

The book on aging was *Good Old Dog—Expert Advice for Keeping Your Aging Dog Happy, Healthy, and Comfortable.*

Chapter 1 includes a comparison age chart for dog years and people years and is reprinted below:[1]

Dog Age in Years	Age Less 20 Lbs.	Age 20–50 Lbs.	Age 5l–90 Lbs.	Age Over 90 Lbs.
8	48	51	59	64
10	56	60	66	78
12	64	69	77	93
14	72	78	88	108
16	80	87	99	123

We joyfully celebrated Brighton's thirteenth birthday on July 4, yet deep in my mind was a whisk of melancholy that I tried to keep hidden. My knowledge of the number thirteen was also affirmed with evidence of age equaling over eighty years.

[1] Dodman, Nicholas, ed. Faculty of the Cummings School of Veterinary Medicine at Tufts University, *Good Old Dog – Expert Advice for Keeping Your Aging Dog Happy, Healthy and Comfortable* (Boston: Houghton Mifflin Harcourt, 2010), 8.

I was on Facebook daily, celebrating golden retriever birthdays with so many others, and especially honoring them with the special achievement of the thirteenth birthday. I even refused in Facebook posts to stress the accomplishment of the elderly age of thirteen as extraordinary. Instead, I would post congratulations and mention that now they had reached the teenage years. It was my participation in a subtle denial of elderly status recognition that many dog owners rightfully choose. There is almost a superstition that if we label our dogs as old, they will reach the end of the line sooner. I found myself answering everyone's question, "How old is Brighton now?" by saying he was thirteen but adding that "he's doing very good." People would say he didn't look that old, and I would feel better that we still had time.

Thirteen, thirteen. Brighton turned thirteen in early July, and a few weeks later, another female golden retriever on Facebook was also celebrating her thirteenth birthday. I posted something cute to the effect that Brighton wished he could come to her PAWty, as they were both thirteen. Brighton ended up meeting a girlfriend in another part of the country who was his age and doing well! Then, a week or so after his girlfriend's thirteenth birthday, she was diagnosed with a liver tumor, and her health was too fragile to warrant surgery. I felt a sense of almost superstition as Brighton and I wished his new girlfriend well in her newly diagnosed medical challenge. It was ironic at that time that we were wishing another thirteen-year-old golden retriever hugs of positive energy and love because within six weeks, Brighton would receive a spleen tumor diagnosis that would actually end his life sooner than his sweetheart. She actually experienced success into her fifteenth year, whereas Brighton died at the age of thirteen years and five months.

Dog lovers will often say they can't stand to read a book or watch a movie if they know the dog dies at the end. Yet, this story is about grief as it equals love. It is meant for those willing to travel the path of grief with me and trust in the inspiration of Brighton's enduring life and spirit!

In the course of Brighton's life, I had joined a number of Facebook groups related to several international golden retriever groups, canine cancer, and rainbow bridge grief support. By the time Brighton had crossed over the rainbow bridge, I had become extremely fond of the members of almost ten groups. Being a highly empathetic person, I was also feeling the heartbreak of others who were dealing with canine cancer and pet grief. I continued to stay with the Facebook groups and post words of sincere compassion and understanding each day. Being that this became a daily review of postings and a regular ministry of condolences, I became extremely aware of the number thirteen. Just as ninety is an age that seems like a bonus lifespan achievement for humans, I realized that the age of thirteen for dogs was a bonus. It confirmed my dread of this benchmark age and the anticipated extreme grief that comes with the eventual rainbow bridge.

My loss of Brighton at the age of thirteen was a blessing in that he lived to that bonus age, but it did not in any way lessen the anguish and grief at his loss. In fact, having him for so many more years than each rabbit, the memories were multiplied three to four times. Plus, the constant intimate contact with Brighton in the home made the loss of that angel in my life like the loss of a piece of my heart. As with the rabbits, I also felt that Brighton could not be replaced, but my heart could find new joy with the emergence of a new dog in our home, Snowdon. I also found that having a second dog like our Snowdon, still in the home when Brighton died was a comfort. I would have been totally lost if I had only had Brighton, although his absence left our home in profound emptiness. Nevertheless, there was still a tremendous void, and our other dog, Snowdon, showed the loss of his constant buddy, as the melancholy continued to permeate our home.

So, it took living through the lifespan ages of my rabbits and my dog, to integrate the deep, profound meaning of the simple number that is the listed lifespan in a pet guidebook. It took continuing my Facebook pet grief ministry to recognize the reality that pet owners choose to avoid. A lifespan number is a guide to the projected life of the dog but is also the reality of the projected death and an unavoidable experience of deep human grief. I have often said, "When you get a dog, you sign up for a broken heart ... but it is worth it."

__SNOW NOW__ (Reflection from Brother Snowdon)

From the day I arrived in my home, Brighton was there. I never had a day when I was without another dog. My life was always with a pack. On Brighton's thirteenth Birthday, Doc took a picture of Brighton and me on the walk around the block. Since it was the Fourth of July, we were both wearing scarves like an American flag. Brighton and I went everywhere together. We didn't always play, as Brighton started to slow down and would walk behind us while I pranced ahead. Yet I lived with assurance in the air that Brighton would always be there.

I have been alone in the house since the day that Brighton passed. I have no competition for attention or treats. I get it all, yet I miss the energy and reassurance of my everyday buddy. It is not the same being alone.

SONG INSPIRATION

At the end of each
chapter, there will
be mention of a song
that was especially meaningful
to the theme expressed in the chapter.

"Dry Your Eyes" (by Neil Diamond)

The summer of Brighton's twelfth birthday, I was given a surprise birthday gift of tickets to Neil Diamond's fiftieth anniversary concert in Houston. There had been a terrible terrorist attack in London a few months before, and Neil Diamond started the concert by singing the beautiful and haunting song "Dry Your Eyes" in honor of those who had been victims of the attack. I had never heard that song before, but it was such a poignant message of mourning for fallen victims.

The message of drying one's tears is so deeply connected to the experience one has in the loss of a pet. I now play this song regularly and watch the online video. There is a message in the lyrics that was manifested in Brighton as he shared his secret about living that stays with me forever. Somehow, dealing with pet loss has forced me to integrate a depth of belief in spirit and life beyond death. How ironic it is that the difference between the word *depth* and *death* is only one letter in the center?

The final line of the song pulls at the grief in my soul, with the profound sadness of the loss of my angel Brighton. The mourning theme of this book is to honor the tears that we shed for our fallen fur angels. No matter when they pass, it is always too soon. By the same token, the integration of the heartache in Brighton's story is designed to comfort readers as they embrace faith in an afterlife.

I feel personally moved every time I hear this message in the song, as it honors the value of every life that has passed.

2

Side By Side

It was a beautiful decade with Brighton by my side. With the reality of his lifespan between ages eleven and twelve, his eleventh birthday was a celebration. Yet it was also a subtle reminder that we had entered the autumn of his life. Although his birthday was on July 4, in the heart of summer, from a benchmark perspective it was definitely nearing fall.

In September, at age eleven, Brighton had his yearly wellness checkup. Dr. P. had operated on Brighton at age six to remove a mast cell tumor. Five years later, Dr. P. warmly greeted Brighton, referring to him as one of his "kids."

"All looks good with Brighton boy. There's some thinning and weakening with his age, and at his rear end here, you can see loss of muscle in his hips," Dr. P. told me.

"Yes, Doc," I said. "He's done so well since his surgery. It's getting more difficult for him to climb the stairs, and we need to help him get into the back of our SUV. He always loves being a couch king, and our large ottoman is his special throne. He's less able to jump up on his favorite spots."

Dr. P then pointed to a tiny bead-sized bump on the underside of Brighton's eyelid. "This little bump should be looked at by a veterinary eye specialist, and I'll give you a referral to Dr. V., who is located in a suburb about thirty minutes from here."

It was a month after Brighton's wellness check that I was scheduled for a major knee replacement surgery. The vet had assured me that his eye needed attention, but not in a hurry. So, I went through with knee replacement surgery in October, followed by painful physical therapy that lasted through the holidays. When Brighton was three, I had eye surgery, and ever since that recovery he had shown a watchful therapy-dog relationship toward me. He again became my quiet comfort during the ten-week period of recovery from knee surgery.

During my recovery, Pops and Brighton became close buddies. Pops took over the walks around the block several times a day. Pops would call for Brighton in the jovial voice he had—like a theatrical circus announcer. Brighton would immediately come, as Pops always had kibble pieces in his pocket as treats. Brighton knew that walks meant treats! In fact, he played the game with Pops so well that during the walks, Brighton would saunter along and then suddenly stop and plant his butt in a sit-down strike. Pops would get frustrated, finally lose patience, and give up by pulling a treat out of his pocket and sighing. Brighton was an expert at managing Pops on walks, as he was the doggone master of begging treats. Pops soon began to call him "beggar!"

Early in January, Brighton had the appointment with the veterinary eye specialist. It was a longer drive in winter weather, and Brighton seemed rightfully uncertain. When we arrived at the clinic, he cautiously peeked out from the hatch of the SUV, looking both ways. Brighton seemed apprehensive, yet curious. He always liked visits to different places. The eye-clinic reception area was long and somewhat narrow with chairs lining the perimeter. Brighton wagged his tail at another dog and owner who were waiting and then sat observing the activity of staff moving back and forth between the other end of the room and the front desk.

Finally, Brighton was taken into an exam room by the sweetest vet he could ever hope to meet. She greeted him by softly saying, "Well, Brighton, look at you, handsome boy."

Dr. V had treats in her pocket, and Brighton immediately wagged his tail and sensed he was making a new friend. This extremely warm vet examined Brighton's eye. She diagnosed the growth as a type of wart that needed to be removed by a minor surgical procedure. Her voice was soft and wise and reassuring, as she described the general ease in the surgical procedure to remove the growth from Brighton's eyelid.

While we were there, I sought her overall assessment of Brighton's health. Dr. V remarked, "For Brighton's age, he looks quite good. I would expect you can be encouraged as to the amount of time he still has with you. I wouldn't write him off too soon."

The eye surgery was held near the end of January, and the removal of the growth went well, with minimal twilight anesthesia to keep him still. Recovery included eye drops several times a day for six weeks. We had been planning to take a winter trip to warmer weather during that time. Pops was sweet and understanding when he heard me explain, "We'll have to postpone our winter vacation as Brighton needs regular monitoring and eye drops for six weeks, and we can't leave him at boarding." Brighton was our boy, and Pops knew no travel could be planned when a family member needed medical care.

Once Brighton's eye had healed from surgery, I had also successfully recovered from a hip and knee replacement, yet I was still limited in the walking that would be required on an alternate trip that Pops had been planning to Europe. Anyone who knew Pops would understand that travel was his lifeline. He flew all over the world as part of his corporate job in global logistics, and international trips had been part of our family's vacation adventures every year.

I was still feeling physically fragile from over two years of using a cane. Plus, with Brighton at almost twelve, I was cherishing every chunk of time I spent with him. I finally felt I was able to relieve Pops from his daily chore of walking both dogs. I therefore insisted that Pops travel on his trip without me. Pops had been so supportive in caring for Brighton and Snowdon, that I felt he deserved the reward of a special trip. Since Pops had traveled internationally on his job for years, travel alone was common for him, and he always had a special excitement for European history and travel by train.

It was while Pops was on his trip in Europe that I had special time with Brighton and Snowdon. Strangely, Brighton started to develop an uncommon habit of barking excessively. I had been getting some physical therapy work done with a movement therapist at that time, and she had known Brighton since he was a pup. I got her permission to bring him along to a private studio session. She would be able to give me her assessment as to the neuromuscular atrophy that seemed to be contributing to Brighton's growing weakness. She did a little muscle release work on his hips and found they were quite tight. Also, at that time she sensed that he may not be hearing very well. Bingo! That was the reason for his new habit of barking! It had become his way of connecting with us. So, at the age of eleven-and-a-half, another sign of declining health due to age became apparent.

In July, we celebrated Brighton's twelfth birthday, and he looked well. He was as beautiful as ever, and although he was a little thinner, it was good that he was not gaining weight with age, as it was helpful in minimizing pressure on his hips. In the back of my mind, the number twelve was a benchmark as to the age that was near the end point of a golden retriever's lifetime.

Brighton had always been terrified of fireworks, and his birthday was on the Fourth of July. Every year since he was a pup, Pops and I would remind ourselves, "Oh, it's two days before the fourth, and there are already fireworks. We can't walk Brighton far from the house. He'll freak if he hears a firecracker while we're walking. We'll have to get him out for a short time early that day so we can be home to comfort him when the booms begin."

On Brighton's twelfth birthday, the Independence Day fireworks were less of a problem. Brighton's hearing was declining, and his barking periods were increasing. We still had to consistently stay home, and we left him alone less in the house with Snowdon. We now had a fear that Brighton might start barking and not stop. It was a worry that he might strain his breathing by getting hoarse without anyone there to stop his compulsive and progressively worsening signal of communication.

INTERNATIONAL GOLDEN RETRIEVER EVENT

A few weeks after Brighton's twelfth birthday, a very special golden retriever event took place in Scotland. It was the celebration of the 150-year anniversary of the golden retriever breed. In 1868, at Guisachan House in Tomich, Scotland, Lord Tweedmouth bred the first litter of golden retrievers. This is one of the most popular dog breeds found today. During the last week of July 2018, 361 golden retrievers and people from thirty-seven countries made a pilgrimage to Scotland to celebrate the golden retriever, its history, and its heritage. Today, all golden retrievers can trace their origins back to Scotland, to the original four puppies of the first litter.

It would have been profound to have attended the anniversary in Scotland, and I did look into the logistics involved. Guisachan House is located near the larger northern city of Inverness in the

Highlands of Scotland. To get there, it would have required travel to Edinburgh or Glasgow and then a number of hours north via train or road travel to Inverness. Instead, I decided to participate as much as I could virtually and watched the online events for five days and shared many of these for others through Facebook. It seemed only fitting that I be home with Brighton and Snowdon, rather than leave them for a week to travel overseas to participate in a golden retriever event without actually bringing a golden retriever.

That September was another yearly wellness check, and Dr. P. carefully examined him. "You can see Brighton's continued slow muscular neuropathy in his hips," he said. "It seems more neuromuscular than caused by arthritis in the joints and bone. Continue using glucosamine supplements to cushion the discomfort coming with age. Also, it looks like Brighton has completely lost his hearing."

Thus, we had the understanding related to the frequent instances of continued barking. Our vet also noted, "The growth seems to be returning to the underside of the same eyelid where he had the eye surgery in January. You should watch it and return to the eye specialist if it continues to grow."

The new wart on Brighton's eyelid did get larger. Again, the following January, we repeated a visit to the eye specialist. She diagnosed the return of the wart and said that it was not uncommon for a recurrence of the wart following surgery. Again, Brighton had a surgical procedure at the end of January that went well. The eye specialist also commented that despite Brighton's age, he looked good, and his bloodwork was fine. Again, we had six weeks of daily eye drops that postponed a planned winter vacation. Yet, Brighton was so special that we were happy to be taking care of our sweet boy.

A general concern for aging dogs is that they experience difficulty in walking because of weakness in the hips that's caused by arthritic progression. Brighton's movement had become more compromised since his eleventh year. We had a two-story home. During my two years of hip and knee replacement, I had set up a padded flat lounge as my sleeping bed in the first-floor family room. Both dogs slept near me while I avoided using stairs as much as possible.

We finally attempted to upgrade my recovery by returning my sleeping arrangement to our large second-floor master bedroom. Brighton had difficulty climbing stairs yet was very fond of the upstairs rooms. Pops was a very strong guy and could lift Brighton to take him upstairs. But this sixty-three-pound golden retriever would flail his back legs and dangerously resist being carried. By Thanksgiving, we decided it was too dangerous for Pops to carry Brighton up the stairs, as both could fall. We again relocated to the main floor of our home.

Brighton had more trouble getting into the hatch area of our SUV. We would intentionally lift him from the cargo area of the SUV to avoid extra pressure on his legs with a long jump down, but Brighton would resist us trying to lift him. Pops would put his strong arms around Brighton's chest, and I would boost him from his rear end. Every time we loaded Brighton into the SUV, it was a major accomplishment, and Pops and I would look at each other and say, "Whew!"

The spring of Brighton's twelfth year was a critical time. We had an extremely important vacation in Europe that had been planned with other family members over a year before. Pops and my son had always had a special interest in World War II. My son had reserved a small apartment in a house in a town located just a few miles from Omaha Beach in Normandy, France. We planned to spend a whole week participating in significant events commemorating the June 6 celebration of the seventy-fifth anniversary of the D-Day Invasion. Airline tickets had been purchased a year in advance, and Pops and I were determined to make arrangements to participate in this once-in-a-lifetime historical experience. We were scheduled to depart the last week in May.

Once Brighton's second eye surgery had successfully healed, I began to experience anguish as to what extraordinary arrangements I could make to provide extended care for Brighton while we were in France. We had the wonderful paws paradise boarding place that Brighton loved to attend regularly for doggie daycare since he was a pup. Whenever he arrived, he would bark enthusiastically and always go into a sit-down strike when I would pick him up to go home. He loved every staff member, and they loved him. Plus, he was there with Snowdon, who would connect with him throughout the entire stay in the open areas where they would spend most of the time. Snowdon and Brighton would also sleep together. Yet, leaving my aging Brighton for sixteen days was a worry for me. Like any owner of a senior dog, I was aware that at the age of almost thirteen, Brighton could be vulnerable at almost any time to the sudden onset of an unexpected, serious medical condition.

We had no family member in our area who would be able to keep Brighton while we were gone. It seemed best to leave him at the paws paradise boarding place he loved, yet I also saw the need to develop an alternate plan for extended care should he develop a medical condition. My extent of intense investigation was incredible. There was an emergency vet hospital just a few miles from the boarding place. I personally checked with them, asking very difficult questions as to what their procedures would be if an emergency occurred and I was out of the country. I would need at least forty-eight hours to fly home from Europe. I was clear with them as to how I would be financially responsible for any procedures and medical boarding required. I assured them that although I was overseas, I would be available at any time by international cell phone.

To investigate all potential arrangements, I also personally visited two other veterinary hospitals near my home that had facilities for medical boarding. In both cases, my personal visit left me uncertain as to an arrangement for twenty-four hour care. I knew I needed to be able to return home within forty-eight hours, should Brighton experience any medical problem. It would break my heart to leave him all alone in such a situation. He could also develop a condition that did not require intensive care, but that did require boarding under constant medical supervision. I began asking other people, trying to find someone who might provide warm and loving care until I would be able to fly home. I finally found a member in my class at the health club who was most compassionate about my worries and would be willing to care for him at home in case of an emergency.

The amount of worry I experienced in preparing for the trip to France is an example of the amount of care we dog owners go through to make proper arrangements for our pets whenever we have plans to travel. You might think I was crazy! In my mind,

I went through the entire scenario of getting a sudden phone call in France, being notified of Brighton developing a medical condition or, even worse, suddenly collapsing. I had investigated the entire train schedule for France, as to how I could suddenly leave Normandy on my own and travel to Brussels to catch a return flight home. The entire timetable worked out that travel could get me back home within forty-eight hours. It was also on my mind what I would do if Brighton died while we were on the trip. It was critical for me to be there for Brighton at the end of his life. My sense of love and loyalty was so profound and geared me to brace myself for the dreaded time when I knew I would have to let Brighton go.

We made the entire trip to Normandy, and it was a profound experience to be along the D-Day Beach coastline for the entire week surrounding June 6 and the anniversary of the D-Day invasion. We were staying in a little apartment in the town of Port-n-Bessin, which had a small harbor less than ten miles east of Omaha Beach. There were American and French flags everywhere and people dressed in army uniforms and riding in vintage D-Day jeeps and other military vehicles. Loudspeakers played music from the 1940s.

We had Wi-Fi in the apartment, and when it was nine in the evening in France, it was two o'clock at home. We would look forward to watching Brighton and Snowdon on the paws kennel "Oh-Doggy" webcam. So delightful! My son would laugh at Pops and me as we would sit at the kitchen table with our eyes glued to the iPad screen, commenting with delight. "Oh, look at Snowdon, cruising the whole area, as usual. Brighton looks happy just resting in the middle of everything, watching the other dogs."

On the actual day of commemoration, we solemnly stood at the American Cemetery at Omaha Beach and listened to memorial speeches by the president of France and the president of the United States. It is impossible to fully describe the sense of spirit that permeated that profound place. We could not stop thinking of how many young soldiers had died on that beach and were buried along the American cemetery's exquisite rows of eternal remembrance. If anything confirms a sense of death, afterlife, and eternal life, it is this place. There are molecules of memory that are felt in the wind and that permeate the moist sea air. No words seem to fit, and the silence is solemn. The year before, on his solo trip to Poland, Pops had solemnly visited several memorial sites to the Holocaust. Now he was silent in prayer and awe at another blood land of World War II. We had seemed to be surrounded by reminders of the mystery of spirit beyond life.

To walk the D-Day beaches, cemetery, and battlefields lined with hedgerows was to step on the hallowed ground of the military land of the rainbow bridge. The years have swept away signs of death from the landscape, but the spirit of patriotism and heroic sacrifice left an essence in my soul that will remain with me forever. That existential synergy with the war has left me with a daunting illusion of grace woven within a subtle breath of death. Yet the spirit in the Normandy landscape became a subtle affirmation that there is life after life. I sometimes wonder if this experience helped me to integrate the spiritual inspiration that I feel has called me to communicate such a message to others through this book!

Sometimes the unspoken dynamics of the universe seems to journey with us through the seasons. Winter brings the shortest day of the year in December, followed by the vernal equinox and faith in spring each March. So was Brighton's life in his final years. Excitement of lengthening days in April and May would crest with the longest day of the year in June, the first day of summer. Days shortened slightly during the months of July and August, and with Brighton's thirteenth birthday in July, the remaining days of his life also began to condense. By the autumnal equinox in September, the dread of the thirteenth year had fulfilled its shrouded prophesy. Brighton's life cycle seemed to be following nature's rhythm of life, death, and new life. In each phase, we were together, side by side.

In July 2020, a new study was published by researchers at University of California San Diego School of Medicine. It throws out the myth that persisted through many years of multiplying your dog's age by seven to calculate how old they are in "human years." A new formula was created that modified the seven ratio over time. When dogs are young, they age rapidly compared to humans. A one-year-old dog is similar to a thirty-year-old human. A four-year-old dog is similar to a fifty-two-year-old human. Then, by seven years old, dog aging slows. An upward-curve line graph is used with dog years on the horizontal and human years on the vertical. Based on the plot of the line graph, age twelve appears to be at seventy in human years, and age fourteen is approaching age seventy-five. This is more encouraging than the old rule-of-thumb 1:7 ratio of age twelve at eighty-four and age fourteen at ninety-eight[2].

SNOW FALL (Snowdon's final months with Brighton)

Brighton was my big brother! From the time I arrived as a little pup, he was always there with me. Brighton was such a calm and gentle guy. I would often be a pest, yet he would always be patient with me, even when I became so annoying that he would just drop and plop and rest. As a little guy, I would sneak up behind Brighton. "Grrrr! Arf, arf! Surprise! I got your furry back end! Ha, ha, ha!" I would say.

We had many years where Brighton and I would wrestle and play hard together, but as I got older and more mature, so did he. It became more difficult for him to get up from the floor. Yet, if Doc yelled, "Brighton, Snowdon, treats!" Brighton would manage

---

[2] Buschman, Heather, "How Old Is Your Dog in Human Years? Scientists Develop Better Method than 'Multiply by 7'." UC San Diego Health, University of California San Diego, July 02, 2020, Accessed 6/8/2022. https://health.ucsd.edu/news/releases/Pages/2020-07-02-how-old-is-your-dog-in-human-years.aspx

to pull himself up hastily and be right there with me! We always, yes always, got the same number of treats, each taking turns.

Treats were Brighton's life, and as he got older, we continued our four walks a day. Pops was such a softie when it came to food! He was always ready for a snack of some kind, and so he treated his doggie boys the same way! Pops always had kibble treats in his pocket, and we could smell them. Brighton would say, "Woof, woof," and would sit intently with his nose aimed right at the treat bulge in Pops's pants. Pops was a very efficient guy, as his job was logistics, and we always got fed by him at the exact same times every day. Walks were always on schedule. He would easily get frustrated at Brighton's sudden halt in the middle of the street and refusal to move until Pops would bring out a reward. Neither of us were very good at listening to a "come" command from Pops, but with the word "treat," we were there!

Brighton always wanted to eat anything he could. Pops would have to watch the ground the whole time we would walk. He'd have to pull hard on the leash before Brighton could grab a piece of goose poop, which he loved! I knew Brighton's trick and would chuckle as he would slow down and get a little out of Doc's sight so he could grab at the gross poop! He also liked to chomp on clumps of loose dirt along the side of the path. It was amazing how fast he could trick Pops and grab an entire mouthful of dirt and sod before Pops could see him. Now me, I am totally a sniffer. As Brighton would eat, I would sniff. We were buddies, but we were different. He was what Doc called a gentleman. I was referred to as a little punk. Despite our differences, we were pals and brothers.

As Brighton got older, he slowed down and had a hard time jumping up on the couch with me and Doc. He always loved his bed, especially his new "my pillow" bed, the one they advertise all the time on TV. I would watch closely with my chin on the floor. As soon as Brighton got up, I would do my "aha" routine and smugly steal his place on the bed! When we would go to doggie daycare or have long staycation times at boarding, we would often sleep in the same suite. During the day in the large play area, I would keep cruising around all day, and Brighton would rest on the side and watch me.

Brighton was always a good boy, and no matter where we were, he would politely let me move in to demand more attention. When guests came to our house, Brighton would greet them with a toy and then quietly lie down to wait a turn to be petted. I would jump and try to hug visitors and make a pest out of myself. In that last year that Brighton was with us, he would suddenly do a strange "woof, woof, woof" routine and would not stop until Doc or Pops would get up to calmly pet him. They would yell, "Brighton, no, stop! Brighton! Brighton!" He could not hear anything they said, and as months went on, Brighton spent more time quietly resting in peace.

Our two-week staycation at paws paradise doggie boarding while Doc and Pops were in France was a memorable time of fun for both of us. They always gave Brighton extra attention because he was older and could not hear. He loved everyone there, and, of course, I tried to move in and be pushy to demand more attention too. We would often be told that Doc and Pops had called from France, and they had said to give each of us a hug.

As Brighton got older, we could not play as much, but I always knew he was there as my buddy, my brother. He was my pack.

SONG INSPIRATION

"By My Side" from the musical *Godspell*

I always loved the musical *Godspell,* and one of my favorite songs is the exquisite slow-moving song with the beautiful message of "By My Side." Somehow this song from long ago is one that I keep the sheet music on my piano. It is my personal reminder of being on a journey in life and having God with me. It is also a reminder of Brighton as my partner.

The song begins questioning a loved one who is leaving and the longing to not be left behind. It makes me think of how I didn't want Brighton to leave. The song continues with sensitive lyrics that truly resonate with my heart, like needing the warmth of the loved one. The lyrics develop toward a horizon, which I see as a metaphor of the rainbow bridge. The song ends with the yearning for the joyful meeting again.

"By My Side" is a metaphorical message of my journey with Brighton throughout his life. We were a team, with Brighton always with me, and, at the end, I was there with him every moment in his final rainbow passage.

3

....

Present Moment

Brighton had been doing fine during the summer after we returned from the D-Day trip to Europe. Three weeks after our return, it was his thirteenth birthday on July 4. We traditionally spent his birthday at home, as the Fourth of July fireworks always frightened him. The fireworks would often start several days before, and it would be precarious to go outdoors. In our neighborhood, fireworks could surprise us any time during the day.

On his thirteenth birthday, Brighton and Snowdon wore red, white, and blue scarves, and the picture that was taken on that day became our last Christmas card that read from both Brighton and Snowdon.

We always found a way to use Brighton's special food from the vet, canned ID, to create his birthday cake. This year, two cans of his ID wet food were arranged in a circle, with one can in the middle surrounded by half cans making a shamrock cake shape. The sides and top were decorated with dry ID kibble. I tried to put out of my mind the thought that this could be Brighton's last birthday, although it loomed in the back of my mind.

Both July and August went well, with Brighton continuing to be slow, especially in walking with the heat of summer sun. He was barking often, yet he enjoyed his peaceful life with his buddy, Snowdon, to entertain him. At the end of July, he was well enough for me to attend a conference that was held out of town. My walking had returned to normal, and I had booked my attendance and presentation and planned to be away for only a few days. Pops had some medical appointments, so Brighton and Snowdon enjoyed a fun staycation break at their paws paradise boarding resort. They enjoyed themselves and reluctantly came home all clean, having been groomed to their English crème golden beauty. Brighton still had such a stunning appearance and did not look his age. Little did we know that this would be his last chance to see his paws paradise family and spend time at his favorite doggie daycare place.

Early in September, I had scheduled Brighton's annual wellness check. Brighton would always prance across the large reception area of the vet clinic with his tail wagging, announcing, "I have arrived!" He would obviously enjoy the smiles from the familiar staff at the counter and savor the attention of letting us position him on the large flat scale to get an accurate reading of his weight.

Brighton was due for a rabies vaccination, but I had concern about his age and weakening condition. Dr. P. has such a soft, welcoming voice and would always greet Brighton as one of his "kids." As the vet outlined the plan for the yearly wellness check, I began to candidly inquire. "Doctor, you know how I've always worried about possible side effects of vaccines. With Brighton's obvious aging, could we have a titer test instead of the vaccination?"

Dr. P. proceeded with a very careful, probing exam. "Brighton's loss of muscle in his hip seems to be a progression of creeping neuropathy. I feel it's not entirely related to age and typical bone-related arthritis. Medications like anti-inflammatories are questionable, as they would provide limited relief. An exact diagnosis can only be made with anesthesia and an X-ray."

I replied, "You know how I want to avoid any anesthesia for Brighton at his age."

I thought the visit was near the end, when Dr. P. continued speaking with hesitation. "Kathy, I'm afraid we have a new issue."

With my hand on Brighton's silky back, I braced for the worst. Dr. P. pointed to the middle of Brighton's lower abdomen area, above his groin.

"I suspect there could be a tumor, possibly on the spleen. The only way to diagnose further would be with an ultrasound."

"Oh no," I said. "Will it require the feared anesthesia?" I was watching Brighton pant with a tiredness that seemed to confirm the suspicious diagnosis.

"No anesthesia is required, but he can't eat the morning of the exam."

"Okay. Whatever you think is best." I sighed. The stress of the test would greatly disturb Brighton's eagerly anticipated morning breakfast each day. Starting a dog's day without breakfast is terrible frustration for both dog and owner.

The ultrasound was scheduled for a few days later. Brighton was not able to eat any breakfast and acted very confused and disturbed at the absence of his beloved kibble. We gave him a much longer early morning walk to keep him distracted outside while Snowdon was fed. Then it was finally time to put Brighton in the SUV. He was left with the vet for the morning portion of the day. Those days of leaving our fur angels with the vet for a day's procedure are times of tremendous trepidation, and the worrying is impossible to fully describe.

In late afternoon on the day of the ultrasound, I had a consultation appointment scheduled with our vet. Dr. P. took me into a darkened back room of the clinic, which had a large-display computer monitor to review ultrasound results. Bless him that he had blocked off a chunk of time to give me the grace of a thorough explanation. Dr. P. proceeded to carefully go over the ultrasound films of the spleen and surrounding abdominal area.

"Kathy, this is the image of the ultrasound. I want you to see it with me on a larger screen. Here is the stomach, intestines, and here is the spleen. You can see there is a distinct tumor attached to the spleen. In looking closer, it appears that the tumor does not invade the other abdominal organs. This could be a cancerous tumor, but there is no way to tell unless we take a biopsy. The only way to confirm cancer is to have the spleen and tumor removed in surgery. There is no other way to remove and analyze a sample of the tumor."

I felt stunned and numb but rationally composed. Questions flooded my head.

"How serious is the surgery? What will happen if the surgery is not done? Based on Brighton's age, what are the expected consequences if we don't have surgery and just let the tumor remain?"

I realized that this type of discussion was so hard for veterinarians, and Dr. P. was obviously using his wealth of experience in being very gentle and calming.

"Kathy, a tumor on the spleen is a life-threatening situation we see in dogs. The only alternatives are surgical removal of spleen and tumor or leaving the tumor, in which case it will grow and eventually rupture and lead to a not seriously painful but sudden death for sure. Right now, the tumor is small enough that it can still be removed without rupture. You could wait a short time to consider the decision, understanding that each week the tumor will grow and get nearer to a point of rupture."

Our vet had known Brighton since he was a pup, and when Brighton was six had conducted surgery to remove a mast cell tumor. Fortunately, clear margins had kept Brighton from further cancer treatment. Dr. P. was being especially calm and compassionate. He knew that he was explaining an eventual end-of-life prognosis. He also knew from the previous surgery experience that I always had many detailed questions, which is why he had scheduled a large block of time where he could explain the alternatives.

"If the tumor and spleen are removed, they will be sent out for biopsy and determination of malignancy. The odds are uncertain, but we could estimate there would be a fifty-fifty chance for the potential of cancer. There's also a chance it could be benign, but age is on the realistic side of cancer diagnosis. If the tumor is malignant, there's a possibility of chemotherapy, however I don't feel it would be something of benefit for Brighton at his age."

My mind was connecting with the worst-case scenario. Brighton had slowed down and been less than vigorous at his age of thirteen. My reaction was to agree that it would be too much to expect him to go through uncomfortable chemotherapy with a potential of buying a very limited amount of extra time.

Our vet therefore left me with three potential choices. "One possible alternative is to have the surgery to remove the tumor and spleen and send the tumor out for biopsy. If the tumor is benign, Brighton would still need recovery from surgery, and then he would hopefully return to his pre-surgery energy level and live out whatever limited months he might have given his aging state. His projected level of time after the surgery would be about three months.

"Another equally possible option would be to have surgery to remove the tumor and spleen, and send the tumor for biopsy, with a result of the biopsy being malignant. This type of cancer is usually a very aggressive form that is called hemangiosarcoma. It generally spreads quite rapidly, and, at most, Brighton would have three additional months of life. Part of that time he would be somewhat compromised as a result of recovery from surgery, since he is already in a weaker aging condition. Also, he may need a transfusion during the surgery, which could not be done in our vet clinic. He would have to be transferred to the emergency vet hospital, where they could also keep him overnight.

"The final option would be to do nothing. This would give Brighton a peaceful end-of-life hospice situation for his remaining days, which would probably be estimated at six to eight weeks. The concern with the third option is that as the tumor continues to grow, it can suddenly reach a point of rupturing and bleeding into the abdomen. This would lead to sudden transport to the clinic with this emergency condition leading to a traumatic death from bleeding out in his abdomen."

I thanked Dr. P. for his clear explanation of the results of the ultrasound and the time he took to compassionately explain Brighton's dreaded prognosis. The nurse was outside in the hallway holding Brighton on his leash and handed him to me, whispering, "I'm sorry."

When we arrived home, there was so much to try to explain to Pops in going over Brighton's diagnosis and serious end-of-life options. Pops and I initially felt we both wanted to give Brighton every chance for more time with us. We felt we couldn't realistically count on the tumor being benign and felt a need to project that it would more than likely be cancer. Yet we still had the faint hope in a miracle that it would be benign. The vet had also explained that even if the tumor was benign, the odds were still that he might only have three months to live, with a slight chance it might be longer. Both Pops and I agonized about wanting to do whatever we could to extend Brighton's time, as being faced with the thought of losing him was sobering and daunting. We decided to call the following morning to schedule surgery for an available date at the end of the next week.

During the lengthy consultation with the vet, I also tactfully asked if there was any other place that might offer specialist treatment for this cancer condition. I was aware of two specialist hospitals within an hour of my home that had been used by some friends for specialized situations. Our vet agreed that we were most welcome to get a second opinion from the specialty hospital, and he would provide us with a referral and X-rays, which he did.

The following day, I called the specialty hospital and made an appointment within a few days for a consultation with a surgeon. The hospital was more than an hour's drive away. A good friend had recently had surgery for her aging golden at that hospital. We were able to get an appointment with the surgeon that my friend had used with a high level of success. Between our vet appointment and the appointment at the specialist hospital, I began to spend hours a day reading online about the spleen tumor and hemangiosarcoma. I talked with others I would find who had already dealt with this condition. It was daunting to integrate the seriousness of the situation and the reality of valuing every day with Brighton, with his end looming on the horizon.

Our appointment at the specialty hospital was with a veteran surgeon who came highly regarded. The hospital dealt specifically with the advanced treatment of specific veterinary conditions. There was a large, open waiting room, as there were a multitude of veterinary specialists on their full-time staff. A framed list on the wall included an extensive list of specialists for cardiology, critical care, dermatology, internal medicine, neurology, oncology, radiation oncology, and surgery.

All of Brighton's blood tests and ultrasound records had been transmitted by Dr. Pf. ahead of time. We first met with a veterinary assistant doctor to go over the situation. The specialist surgeon entered and immediately provided an impression of expertise, combined with a genuine interest in Brighton and the importance of this examination. Brighton was a "good boy" patient and stood still, somehow showing trust that we were all interested in his best care. The specialist surgeon directed me to walk Brighton down the hallway as he carefully observed his stride and general level of mobility. The surgeon then provided a thorough analysis.

"Brighton shows good mobility in his walking, which is a positive sign. I see that Dr. P. has provided you with basic prognosis information about the ultrasound showing a typical tumor on the spleen. At this time, the tumor is not too large, and Brighton could be a candidate for a successful removal of the tumor and spleen. There's no way of knowing if the tumor is malignant unless it's removed and biopsied."

I asked very candidly, "What do you see as his chances of making it through the surgery and a satisfactory recovery? How much time would we have to make the decision?"

The surgeon explained additional details to help us with a decision. "You would bring Brighton in early on the morning of surgery. We would do final bloodwork, and I do all the surgeries in the afternoon. An advantage of having the surgery here versus at a regular clinic is that we have immediate access to blood transfusions both during and following the surgery. Also, he would be kept here at the hospital in intensive care for two nights to have his recovery closely monitored."

The thought of having immediate access to a blood transfusion seemed to be a definite advantage, as well as having him monitored afterward in intensive care. If the surgery was done at our regular clinic, they would not have access to a blood transfusion. Plus, they were not open overnight at the regular clinic, and I would have to bring him home after six o'clock on the day of surgery. I would then be totally responsible for all his post-surgery care. That thought made me extremely anxious. If anything went wrong, I would be responsible for saving his life! I knew my guilt would be profound if Brighton were to have any life-threatening emergency situations on my watch.

The specialty surgeon finally confirmed our vet's prognosis. The projection of three-month's survival with surgery and a malignant tumor was again clarified. Also, even with a benign tumor, the projected survival seemed not significantly longer between the recovery time from surgery and his thirteen-year-old age factor.

We were again given the option of not doing anything. However, there was a clear warning of the continued growth of the tumor and potential traumatic rupture at any time. Therefore, both the vet and the surgeon did recommended surgery be done as soon as possible, before the tumor grew more or possibly ruptured. The surgeon said we could wait perhaps a week to decide but would not suggest waiting much longer.

During the entire visit at the specialty hospital, Brighton was such a good patient. There were several dogs in the large waiting room, and he was curious and even politely wagged his tail and tried to connect with other people and dogs. In the exam room, he was very patient and extremely trusting. Bless him! He could sense we were all looking out for him, and besides, he had always loved any kind of a gig for something new. Throughout his life, he had been taken many places, including doing some therapy work visits. He was truly a good boy and deserved the very best care in all the decisions we made for him. Everyone had maintained a warm, caring, yet highly intelligent demeanor throughout the visit and discussions.

The long drive on the way home from the specialty hospital gave both Pops and me a lot of time to brainstorm the advantages and consequences of our decision for Brighton. Pops was always the strong, silent partner, who quietly remarked that the specialty hospital was "good." It was hard for either of us to express the circumstances of the decision that would lead to Brighton's death.

I felt discouraged and said, "None of the options provide a projection that would give Brighton an extended amount of time with us. I personally feel it would be a challenge for us to drive over an hour in rush hour traffic to the specialty hospital for the day of the surgery. I also have a hard time thinking of him in ICU for two nights with total strangers. I worry about him feeling alone without being able to see us. On the contrary, I do feel reassured that he would have intensive medical care for two days following surgery, plus a blood transfusion would be readily available if needed."

Frankly, I was also experiencing a lot of anxiety at the thought of having to take him home the day of surgery from our regular vet and being totally responsible for his postoperative care. Another issue that concerned me was the possible blood transfusion. I explained this to Pops. "If, as a result of the surgery, Brighton needed a transfusion, the specialty hospital would be able to facilitate that right during the surgery. If he needed a transfusion with our vet, we would need to transport him to another veterinary hospital that had a setup for transfusion. The cost is not a factor in our decision, of course. We have pet insurance that covers a portion of the medical costs in either scenario."

By the evening of the specialty hospital visit, I was in favor of the long-distance facility, as I felt totally inadequate having the complete responsibility for immediate postoperative care placed on my shoulders. If Brighton were to die at home under my postoperative care, I would never get over the failure to save his life.

Pops never liked driving long distances, especially in a lot of expressway traffic. His field was logistics, which was always finding the quickest and most efficient way to get from point A to point B. For years, he had a job that forced him to spend an hour to work and back—each way—on a crowded expressway. He had no patience for such a ride under normal circumstances, much less in transporting our beloved Brighton for life-threatening surgery. It was beyond his boundaries to endure. So, during the long ride home, Pops was his quiet self, but later shared a firm opinion.

"It's better for Brighton to be with our own vet and with people who personally care about him and who would do everything to save him," he said. "I'm totally against the specialty hospital. It's comforting for Brighton not to be driven so far away, where he would be kept in the hospital with total strangers for two days following surgery. I don't want him so far away with total strangers. We've had complete trust in Dr. P. I'm loyal to our own vet, and I know he'll do the very best possible with the surgery. Plus, everyone at our vet clinic has been giving such personal attention to Brighton for thirteen years."

We had told the specialty hospital that we would get back to them within a day or two if we wanted to get Brighton on the surgery schedule. At the same time, three days from the appointment, we had already scheduled the surgery to be done by our own veterinarian, Dr. P.

I spent the next two days in pure agony, pondering what was best for Brighton. Pops had been adamant in his decision that it was best to have the surgery done by our own vet. It would be closer to home, where Brighton could be brought home for our immediate close attention and care. I knew we had the surgery date scheduled with our home vet for Friday. I admit I was truly in anguish at the thought of bringing my baby home from surgery the same day. My mind was going to the worst-case scenario, with a deep fear of being totally responsible for Brighton's post-surgery life. Plus, I worried about the possibility of rushing him to another hospital for a transfusion. I could not bear the thought of having him go into post-surgery crisis and me being the only one there to save him. The thought of losing him under my watch was more than I could bear and more than I could ever live with, should it happen.

Pops was a very practical retired businessman and problem-solver. He felt confident in having the surgery done by our highly competent home vet. Plus, Pops had more confidence in me than I had in myself. He felt that I could handle any situation in Brighton's post-surgery care. I admit I was the ultimate dog-owner worrier who had spent days researching the worst-case scenario. Embedded in my soul was the fear of dealing with death again, as had been my reality with my numerous bunnies years before. Pops was always so competently pragmatic!

A further thought surrounded the surgery scenario in the fixation on the three-month mark that seemed to haunt any of the decisions. Regardless of surgery, it seemed the likelihood was a prognosis of three months. Plus, with the surgery, I expected our aging Brighton to have at least two weeks of discomfort and added care in postop recovery. He would certainly be compromised in terms of recovery from anesthesia, likely needing a cone around his head, have a healing of surgical site, and the inability to regain his already aging energy level. I felt recovery from surgery would leave us with perhaps ten weeks of returning to gradual decline in activity; however, he might never completely regain his limited energy. If we declined the surgery, the prognosis was six to eight weeks, but there would be no trauma from surgery or recovery. If we were able to extend to Brighton a peaceful hospice prognosis beyond the eight-week marker, we could equal the amount of quality of life he would have, if we went ahead with the surgery. What was the advantage?

The anxiety over the surgery decision tore at my heart and soul, as I know it does with every surgery decision. I had literally gotten myself overwhelmed by the early morning of the day before surgery. I felt a panic that I could not go ahead with the surgery with our home vet, as it would put me in the role of being Brighton's life-sustaining intensive care nurse afterward. Plus, I had become more convinced that declining the surgery would provide our dear Brighton with the immediate peace and tender care from now until his uncertain end. It suddenly became clear to me what was best for Brighton!

I was in my car having coffee early in the morning prior to the scheduled surgery. With total fear and trepidation, I realized that

I felt an urgent need to make an impulsive decision to call our vet when they opened. This is an example of the emotional stress that accompanies the decisions for this type of end-of-life surgery. I knew it would be disloyal to Pops to make such a decision to cancel the surgery myself. Yet, I was afraid that if I went home to discuss it, it would only lead to a heated argument with Pops. One of Pops' highest traits is loyalty, and he would be loyal to our home vet and to the commitment we made for surgery the following day.

I felt totally petrified with my audacity to make a controversial decision to cancel, and I knew that Pops would be extremely furious at my disloyalty in not including him in the decision. I also knew that Pops has a personal policy to never cancel anything once a decision is made. We both loved Brighton, and it was only right to mutually discuss any of these final decisions on his life. Yet, I was so driven by the anxiety and sense of urgency that I could not wait any longer! So, I intuitively made a gut-wrenching call to the vet office to tell them I was canceling the surgery on the following day. I told them we had decided to consider surgery only with the additional ICU post-surgery support of the specialty hospital.

My anxiety and guilt were overwhelming. I had no right to exclude Pops in making such a life-threatening decision. Now I had the further trauma of facing his anger for cancelling the scheduled surgery without his approval. I was terribly frightened to tell him, and I cowardly sent him a text admitting what I had done. Yet there was more than an apology needed for making the cancellation decision myself rather than attempting to discuss it. It shows the deep level of emotional trauma that arises when the laws of reasonable communication are violated. Our relationship was being severely damaged in the decision.

As expected, Pops reacted with vehement anger at my action and sent a return text saying, "I'm appalled that you would cancel the surgery without consulting me."

The result of my disloyalty to Pops created one of the worst confrontations we had ever experienced, and I knew it was my fault. With the surgery cancelled, it took twenty-four hours of frigid silence before I could even face Pops in attempt to apologize. It also seemed my anxiety and fear of the surgery had been multiplied by a tremendous anxiety and fear of the strength and decisiveness of Pops. Finally, when I tried to break the ice with Pops, he shouted in an angry face-to-face retort.

"We are *not* going to have the surgery at the specialty hospital! In fact, we are *not* going to have the surgery at all!"

I admitted that when I had made the call to cancel the surgery with Dr. P., I still had in the back of my mind the option of possibly considering the specialty hospital. Now, I realized Brighton's surgery decision was figuratively "carved in stone."

"Okay," I humbly said. "So be it."

What I did not realize in my agony over the surgery decision was that at the same time, Pops had also been agonizing over a possible cancellation. The following day, we were finally able to bridge our personal wounds, sit down, and talk. Pops rightfully chastised me. "I'm so appalled that you didn't discuss cancelling with me. I've also been haunted with second thoughts about what's best for Brighton. I realized we were being selfish by putting him through surgery and the discomfort afterward, with the possibility of perhaps gaining a few extra days for us. I don't think Brighton would want that. He was always so gentle and peaceful. The more I thought about it, the more I realized peaceful days of hospice care is best for him, giving him love and comfort from now until his end of days," he said.

There was such an irony in the tremendous discord created by the surgery decision. It was fueled by a battle of conflicting loyalty. I felt loyal to our vet, yet I was embarrassed in my need to cancel the surgery at the last moment. It was out of my deep love and loyalty toward Brighton. In the process, I hurt Pops. Plus, Pops had a deep loyalty to Brighton to do everything to give him life. What became the juncture of healing the subsequent hurt was our deep love and loyalty toward Brighton. What is also clearly shown is the trepidation and anxiety around surgery. It is important for both parents to be honored equally in making such a life-threatening decision. Truly a dog is a cherished member of the family that everyone loves.

Suddenly our love for Brighton had brought Pops and me back together. We agreed it did not seem fair to give Brighton the trauma of anesthesia and surgery, with a tenuous post-op at home, and the discomfort of recovering from surgery. We both expressed the fear that with Brighton's weaker energy level and age, it might be asking too much of our sweet boy to regain his already limited state and recover with an ability to move and function. We were perhaps being too centered on our own fear of loss, rather than on what sweet Brighton would have preferred. Somehow our love for Brighton brought us the grace we needed to make this decision.

On Friday evening, the night of the cancelled surgery, Pops and I finally sat down and had a long talk. We mutually agreed to make hospice the choice in this end-of-life journey for our sweet

Brighton. We both loved him so much and were now speaking from our hearts and doing what was best for him. It was a relief to feel at peace in doing the best for our sweet angel boy. That same night, we began to project an open plan for the next three months.

It was our total intent to give Brighton an outpouring of love and care in the *present moment* of each day. It just felt right for Brighton to let him be himself. We had truly embarked on the lifelong lesson for all of us to live totally in the *present moment*, the final gift that was to be Brighton's divine legacy.

<u>SNOW KIDDING</u> (Snowdon's Doggone Wisdom)

Snowdon was the silent partner in the *now do* scenario of our home. (Notice the *now do* is in the middle of my name, **SNOW-DON**).

He was mumbling, "Boy, is there a lot of drama at our house! For the first time ever, I was left at paws paradise, but Brighton was not there with me. That was strange, but I just enjoyed my carefree playtime, like I always do."

Snowdon went on with his silent observations. "For the next week, I could feel a ton of tension in the house between Doc and Pops, like a wall of ice! Brighton just went on, resting quietly. Since he had lost his hearing, he was our resident wise old Yoda. He knew how to snooze better than anyone and loved resting by the patio door, looking out at the trees and the pond beyond our deck."

Snowdon noticed the difference in each present moment at home.

"I had to get used to being more on my own. Each week, Brighton is less able to play with me, and I kept being reminded to calm down. It was weird how Brighton had regular spells of sudden barking without stopping. He couldn't hear any more, so Doc would suddenly get up and give him eye contact and use a hand signal to get him to stop. We all needed to be sure Brighton could see us, as he couldn't hear us at all."

Snowdon was making subtle adjustments in so many ways.

"Brighton had more trouble getting up on his back legs. When it was time to go out, Doc and Pops had to get their hands under his backside and lift up his rear end. Once Brighton got going on his walk, he was fine but slow and tagged along behind Doc or Pops. I pranced ahead like a trailblazer, sniffing all the doggie smells. Brighton still pulled his beggar man trick and suddenly stopped in the middle of the street. He did a solid stall where he wouldn't move until lured by a treat. Brighton always played a stubborn game of refusing to do things unless he was given the bait of a treat. They always said that Brighton was food driven. No kidding!"

Brighton was still tricky in the house whenever it came to food.

"Ha! Brighton looked like he was resting on his bed or the floor. I went to Pops to beg for a treat, which Pops always had in his pants pocket. Brighton may have looked like he was sleeping, but he suddenly perked up and made a huge effort to get his back end up so he got an equal share of treats! We always had treat distribution in turns—one for me, one for Brighton, and back and forth."

Snowdon continued to observe changes in our family. He sensed this especially during one particular week.

"Boy, something is really up this week!" he said. "The whole energy of the house is tense, sharp, and unhappy. Doc and Pops are not talking to each other."

Snowdon was now feeling that home life was all about Brighton.

"Now, I'm watching out for Brighton, when through my whole life he has been watching me. I miss us being able to wrestle. Now when I try to playfully mount Brighton's rear end after I get done eating, Pops says, 'Snowman, no!' to my annoying boyish behavior. It is now totally out of bounds. We're all especially careful about Brighton's rear end, and his ability to walk around the block is not normal anymore. Now, Doc makes a big deal to celebrate his fancy way of slowly walking like a prince! Snow kidding!"

SONG INSPIRATION

"Nothin' but a Heartache" (by Neil Diamond)

In writing this book, a song by pure synchronicity came into my sphere of hearing. I had never heard the song before, yet in playing a Neil Diamond CD, the song "Nothin' but a Heartache" attacked my heartstrings! It is sung very slowly, with each word evolving within a story of heartache and rescue.

In the hospice journey of Brighton's life, I was living one moment at a time, trying to overpower and comfort my heartache with the overwhelming existence of hope, faith and love. Heartache became the bass string in the guitar of my life. The lyrics of the song reverberated in me like a creeping arpeggio. Many significant words and phrases directly plucked at my buried feelings. This synchronistic song helped me to express the emerging requiem that I felt as Brighton's rainbow bridge journey drew near.

The loss of Brighton was certainly "nothin' but a heartache" and described the experience of an awful dream. How true are the lyrics that refer to going down an uncertain road with a long-awaited exit. It is a journey of heartache where one can't walk away. The song ends with an inspiring reflection of the two of us together forever. It is faith that nurtures each present moment of heartache as a stepping-stone in the forever rainbow journey.

4

··

Hope, Faith, Love

Once we had made a thoughtful decision to decline surgery for Brighton, our mindset became a focus on peace. We had a three-month framework in mind and dynamic care within a totally loving hospice situation. Throughout the days of decisions and second opinions, our connection with Brighton was in a spirit of love. Every time we fed him, petted him, or walked him, it was a focus on the moment and savoring the love we were sharing every minute of our day.

In weeks of hospice that followed, we stayed home almost all the time, or one would go out and the other would stay. I cancelled going to a workout class at the health club and a monthly seminar that would take me away from home for half a day. I wanted to spend every possible moment at home with Brighton. Also, with his hearing issue, he would suddenly start to bark consistently for long periods. I feared that if we were not home, he would start to bark and not stop and exhaust his lungs. He would move around the house and snooze in his favorite places, and I would read or do some paperwork or quiet housework where he could calmly know that I was near.

In reading about the aging of dogs, I learned that they forget when a potty break is needed. We began to be on regular alert for a time when he would get up and start to move in an uncertain direction, learning it was a signal he was ready to poop. If we could catch him and rush him out, we did. If it happened too quickly, we had paper towels, disinfectant, and plastic bags to wipe things up in less than a minute, while he would quietly watch with a puzzled reaction. I would calm him and say, "It's okay," and distract him from what had happened. Our goal was to read his mind and think ahead to limit embarrassing moments. It was much easier to be in the house to anticipate Brighton's unexpected needs.

A lot of the time in the weeks following his diagnosis involved researching the internet for more information about spleen tumors, canine cancer, and learning the severity of the word *hemangiosarcoma*. I became more knowledgeable about hemangiosarcoma, learning that it is a most-aggressive, invasive cancer that arises from the blood cells and typically affects the spleen. The term was mentioned to me many times during the first week after his diagnosis, but it took a long time for me to fully connect with the word and integrate pronunciation, spelling, and meaning.

I had been a member of several golden retriever Facebook groups and soon was led to join other groups related to canine cancer and hemangiosarcoma. These sites often included the sad reporting of time running out for dogs dealing with canine cancer. I also connected with several Facebook groups related to the rainbow bridge and pet grief. It was all my reality now and part of our family's final journey with Brighton.

The hemangiosarcoma Facebook groups were extremely supportive and unbelievably helpful. Everyone in the groups was struggling with this ticking time bomb and were giving tenacious and Herculean efforts to extend the lives of their pets. I learned that many alternative herbs and products were being used in the effort to shrink or inhibit the growth of the tumor. All efforts went to provide overall support for health in battling this ongoing disease. It was overwhelming to read all the resources that were recommended. Products being used included:

1. Yunnan Baiyao to prevent bleeds. This is a proprietary traditional Chinese medicine marketed and used as an alternative hemostatic product in both human and veterinary alternative medicine. The Yunnan Baiyao package includes a little red pill to be used in case of emergency collapse from severe bleeds.

2. I'm-Yunity for dogs. I'm-Yunity is an extract that contains the standardized ingredient polysaccharopeptide (PSP), which can be isolated only from the proprietary strain (COV-1) of the *Coriolus versicolor* mushroom. This proprietary extract has been clinically proven to support the immune system, reduce chronic and acute pain, and improve appetite, stamina, and maintain general well-being. The serving size is one capsule (400 mg). The PSP content is not less than 38 percent. The dosage is 100 mg per 1 kg of the dog's

body weight per day. So, sixty-two-pound weight would mean seven capsules per day, divided into two equal doses taken with morning and evening meals. For more information, see Imyunityfordogs.com or call Horizon Life Sciences at (866-932-9993).

3. CBD oil—Cannabidiol (CBD) is a phytocannabinoid, first discovered in 1940. It is one of 113 identified cannabinoids in cannabis plants and accounts for up to 40 percent of the plant's extract. As of 2019, clinical research on CBD included studies of anxiety, cognition, movement disorders, and pain. CBD oil is becoming more popular in nonprescriptive usage.

After extensive research and discussions with others on Facebook, I felt there was enough support for Yunnan Baiyao and I'm-Yunity for me to discuss use of these herbal supplements with my vet. I felt total support and compassion from our vet and wanted to clear any alternative products we used. I learned that, at times, vets use Yunnan Baiyao to control bleeding, and this herbal product was kept as part of the pharmacy supply at our veterinary clinic. My vet acquiesced to prescribing the Yunnan Baiyao. Because of limited supply on hand, I needed to notify them ahead of time if I would be in need of a refill.

Our vet did not use or carry a supply of I'm-Yunnity but was aware of the herbal product and gave approval for us to make a choice on our own to order and add it to our hospice treatment plan. I had to order the I'm-Yunity directly from the manufacturer and place a rush order on this very expensive product.

At the time of the wellness check, the vet had prescribed

Vetprofen, an anti-inflammatory for control of arthritic pain. That was also to be continued.

We had reached the second week in October, a few weeks after initial diagnosis, second opinion, and further research consultation with our vet. I was ready to start the use of the herbal treatment products. On Friday, I began the Yunnan Baiyao. The rush order of I'm-Yunity arrived on Saturday, and I administered it immediately upon arrival. I carefully followed the directions for administration and hoped it was helping to buy a little more time.

By Sunday, Brighton had developed a concerning lethargy and was also developing a loose stool. Brighton's condition had declined significantly by Monday. He was moving around with bouts of sudden diarrhea, to the point of barely being able to get up. He had soiled himself, and I had to devise a way to prop up his weak front chest on a stool, while placing his rear end into a dishpan to bathe and clean him. My poor boy!

First thing on Monday morning, I made an appointment to see our vet on Tuesday, and Brighton continued to decline and just rest on a towel on his bed in the hallway. He would not eat and had runny stool and no energy. He was sleeping and slipping throughout Monday. I spent several hours in tears, fearful that we had already reached the dreaded time for putting him to sleep at the appointment on Tuesday morning.

Brighton continued in this totally weakened state throughout Monday night. On Tuesday morning, we had to lift him to get him into our SUV. When we reached the vet, we parked right in front of the door and were able to get him to slowly walk into the lobby. I still sadly remember slowly guiding him into the lobby and toward the floor scale. Right in the middle of the lobby, he stopped and soiled a large spot on the tile floor. The nurses were so sweet to us and got him right into an exam room and cleaned everything in a flash, assuring us that they deal with these things all the time. I knew better.

When Dr. P. came into the exam room, he carefully palpated the abdominal area and said he did not feel the tumor had grown significantly. He did not think Brighton was in a rupture situation leading to internal bleeding, but the severe diarrhea was definitely taking him down. For years, Brighton had dealt with a food allergy that we kept under control with a digestive supplement, and his only food or treats were a prescriptive canned ID food and kibble. Years before, he had dealt with severe diarrhea that had been under complete management until now.

We discussed with the vet whether the tumor was already taking him down or if management of the diarrhea could pull him out of this serious malaise. I then discussed that we had just started the Yunnan Baiyao and I'm-Yunity herbal supplements, and we realized that the severe disturbance was being caused by a reaction to the strength of these medications.

Our vet was extremely compassionate. "We still have a chance to rescue Brighton through intense treatment of the diarrhea," he said. "We'll take him off all medications, such as the pet anti-inflammatory, and discontinue the regimen of Chinese herbal supplements. His diet will be adjusted to discontinue his ID dog food and switch to organic cooked chicken for the most protein. Then you can introduce canned pumpkin. It is the best way to turn around his severe digestive condition. I'll also add a prescription of metronidazole to specifically address the diarrhea."

We left the clinic with Brighton and a renewed hope that perhaps he was not yet ready for the rainbow bridge.

The severe situation that almost led to loss of Brighton became an intense wake-up call. Our sweet boy was definitely on a downward slide that might be slowed, but not reversed. We had reached a point that weekend where he could not walk. It made me aware of other strategies that would support him in comfort during his hospice time and final decline. Pops had an old-fashioned red wagon in our garage that had not been used for years. I spent several hours cleaning it and lining it with a foam cushion. The wagon stayed in our garage, ready for use at any time. If we were on one of our short walks with Brighton and he happened to collapse or become unable to walk, we would be ready to rush home and get the wagon. We also had a ready supply of puppy pads, disinfectant wipes, paper towels, plastic bags, a dishpan, gentle shampoo, and wipes I found at the pet store that can be used as a substitute for complete bathing.

Brighton's severe digestive disorder did resolve within a week after using the metronidazole for the diarrhea and discontinuing the Chinese herbs and Vetprofen anti-inflammatory medicine. His regular diet became a focus on high-quality protein with an intense caution for the severe food allergies that he had experienced his whole life. He was given as much organic cooked chicken as he would eat, combined with pure canned pumpkin to manage his fragile digestive system. We had tried to continue his ID dog food, but once he became accustomed to the delicacy of the expensive organic chicken breast, he refused his standard food and insisted that chicken breast become his staple.

I continued to follow the canine cancer postings on Facebook about alternative supplementation with Chinese herbs and other suggested regimes. However, I realized with Brighton's delicate food sensitivities that our best investment for him was to keep his food and medication simple. It was important to avoid any further diarrhea that we knew could easily take him down. Later, I learned that starting Brighton on the recommended dose of the Yunnan Baiyao and I'm-Yunity was too much and should have been introduced gradually.

Frankly, I do not feel there would have been a significant change in the results had I continued the Chinese herbs in gradual portions. The Yunnan Baiyao was to prevent bleeds, and we never experienced a rupture-and-bleed emergency situation where we would have needed the red pill.

The hemangiosarcoma Facebook group had also referred me to Dr. Mark J. Mamula, a professor of medicine at Yale School of Medicine. He has been doing a research study on the epidermal growth factor receptor peptide vaccination induces cross-reactive immunity to human EGFT, HER2, and HER3, published online in 2018. The research study continues with the use of an experimental therapy to examine the ability of dogs to develop antitumor immune responses after vaccination. The vaccination utilizes a group of proteins, known as EGFR and HER2, that are overexpressed in a variety of human and dog tumors that are typically associated with more progressive diseases and a worse outcome.[3]

---

[3] Doyle, Hester A., Koski, Raymond A., Bonafe, Nathalie, Bruck, Ross A., Tagliatela, Stephanie M., Gee, Renelle J., Mamula, Mark J. "Epidermal growth factor receptor peptide vaccination induces cross-reactive immunity to human EGFR, HER2, and HER3, Cancer immunology, immunotherapy (2018) 67: 1559-1569, https://doi.org/10.1007/s00262-018-2218-9.

In early October, I received specific information about considering participation in the research study. Brighton would receive two injections of the vaccine approximately twenty-one days apart. A small amount of blood would be collected before vaccination and twice after vaccination. The purpose of the study was to determine whether the vaccine elicits immune responses that reduce the tumor. If we were to participate in the research study, our personal veterinarian would remain the primary care provider for our pet.

After carefully reviewing the research paper and information provided via email from Dr. Mamula, I consulted with Dr. P. Our vet would need to become a participant in the study as well, and that would take considerable time. Also, most of the participants in the study had the tumor removed, where we had decided on nonsurgical palliative care. Imaging would have to be used in our case to track growth. Brighton had a history of allergic responses to food, plus several instances of seizures, which made the precautions in our case outweigh any uncertain potential benefit. We therefore declined participation in the study, but it was an example of the delicate balance that is the reality between treatment and palliative care in a normally fatal hemangiosarcoma prognosis.

By mid-October, we had already faced a situation leading to thought of euthanasia due to sudden severe decline from the diarrhea. It became expedient for me to prepare in the best way possible for Brighton's continued decline, comfort, and eventual passage. I had wanted to avoid the typical scenario of having to take him to our vet for his final journey to be put to sleep at the vet's office. I had once been in the comfort room at the vet clinic with a separate door where the dignity of euthanasia was maintained. I had left that room with a residual feeling that it was not where I wanted to say good-bye to Brighton when the time came. I could not imagine walking out of that side door and leaving Brighton there to be collected later and transported with other bodies to the pet cemetery. The scenario haunted me with a horrible sense of dread. (How ironic that is the similarity between the words *dread* and *dead*!)

Once Brighton's condition had stabilized, I began to seek a vet who could administer euthanasia in our home. I did an online search and was able to find an at-home vet who was located about forty-five minutes from my home. Her specialty was hospice care, but her hospice caseload was full. She did say that when the time came, she could be contacted for an appointment for euthanasia in my home. It was a compassionate exchange, but I did not feel that I had the security I wanted in the course of strong support along this part of the hospice journey.

I continued to ask others to see if I could find a more strongly confirmed home hospice arrangement. Totally by coincidence, I had a good friend who worked on the staff of another vet clinic. She mentioned that in the previous year, there had been a vet who regularly came to their veterinary clinic in connection with specific hospice arrangements, but that vet was no longer visiting their clinic. She gave me the vet's name, and I made contact. What resulted was truly a coincidence leading to an angel arrangement.

When I made contact with Dr. M., I found that she mainly handled hospice treatment and supervision, plus in-home euthanasia. Also, I learned that her hospice support included acupuncture. That was of special interest to me, as I myself had, over the years, had experience in using various alternative homeopathic health therapies. I had become familiar with acupuncture, chiropractic, massage, reiki, and more. I knew right away that I would use acupuncture as another support therapy for Brighton. Dr. M. explained that an initial at-home visit would be a two-hour physical exam plus an extensive consultation. This was exactly what I wanted, so I could get a deep understanding of the best way to support Brighton along this path and through his final journey. She would also review complete copies of his medical records for a holistic perspective.

The first appointment with Dr. M. was so rewarding for Brighton and for me. I had no idea what to expect. When she arrived at the door, both Brighton and Snowdon were excited at the new visitor. Plus, Dr. M. was a lovely young woman with a very warm and friendly demeanor. Snowdon was thrilled, and I had to put him aside so the visit could be totally directed toward Brighton. I had Brighton recline on his big dog bed in the foyer, and Dr. M. casually knelt beside him and began to carefully stroke him and examine his body parts. It was obvious that Brighton felt a warmth and complete sense of care from Dr. M.

There was an extensive checklist form that was used to assess Brighton's condition. It covered his medical history and current characteristics. Dr. M. took careful notes at each point of the exam and used the assessment as a prescription for points to use in the administration of acupuncture. It was amazing how quietly Brighton reclined on his dog bed while Dr. M. inserted extremely long, thin needles into various points in his body. He was such a sweet and calm and cooperate patient, and it was obvious that he loved Dr. M.

During the exam and acupuncture treatment, I positioned myself far enough away so as not to distract Brighton. I had also worked to keep the entire area of the house quiet and peaceful, and that included keeping Snowdon close and restrained. Snowdon was very curious but was still watching with his chin on the floor, knowing he could be allowed to observe only if he stayed very quiet.

I also had to control my own excitement. There was a need for me to refrain from talking constantly and to give Dr. M. the quiet and space to make the most important acupuncture connection directly with Brighton. I find one of my faults with vet appointments is that I often do not stop talking. I have realized it is better to let the vet take over and to provide quiet to allow kinesthetic connection with the patient.

Once Dr. M. had finished the lengthy initial exam and acupuncture procedure, I was available to share additional information with her. I had learned quite a bit of detail from the hemangiosarcoma Facebook groups, as well as from my own vet, and from the surgeon's second opinion at the specialty hospital. Dr. M.'s review of Brighton's condition did not raise any significant questions, and she reviewed a helpful scale with categories for quality of life. Her extensive exam and review of the records confirmed the status of the situation and the decision to support palliative care, which I refer to as hospice. Brighton's most recent, severe situation with diarrhea had affirmed his lifelong food allergy. It was agreed that the Chinese herb regime may have been too much for Brighton's delicate digestive system to tolerate.

Dr. M. provided information about Brighton's hospice situation in his journey to eventual need for euthanasia. She said, "You can review the quality-of-life checklist items each week to monitor his symptoms and note when they become more serious. I can make regular scheduled home visits to continue acupuncture treatment. Plus, I'll be on call for phone guidance in an emergency situation. If I'm unable to immediately come to the home for an emergency, I would provide advice as to seeking other local twenty-four-hour emergency care. The understanding, of course, is not length of life when you are in a hospice situation. The goal is comfort and lack of suffering in the course of impending death."

My mind was clouded with emotion in the discussion of plans for Brighton's passing. I asked Dr. M. to repeat her instructions as she handed me a folder with a written handout.

In relief, I said, "Oh, thank you for providing everything in writing. This is hard for me to digest, and I'm so worried, wanting to do things correctly."

Dr. M. went a little further in seeing that I needed more assurance. She explained, "I can prescribe an at-home kit that will include several syringes of tranquilizer and a strong pain killer. I'll train you to administer injections in an emergency situation."

This additional emergency safeguard provided me with genuine comfort.

The initial visit with Dr. M. had been scheduled for two hours. There was the one-hour examination, assessment, and then approximately forty minutes for the first acupuncture treatment. The second hour was spent going over the initial exam, patient history, extensive assessment, and training in the regular use of the quality-of-life checklist. The final ten minutes were spent giving some personal attention to Snowdon, who had been patiently waiting, and setting up a schedule of appointments starting with twice-a-week and eventually once-a-week or as-needed visits.

Dr. M.'s next several home visits were to provide acupuncture for Brighton in an effort to perhaps strengthen his overall "chi" and energy to perhaps extend his life. At least it would provide him with consistent comfort, monitoring, and peace.

Brighton was the star in this hospice drama, yet for him, it was like a silent movie. He could not hear and mainly seemed to enjoy resting and snoozing. He would choose to relax on his dog bed in the foyer, looking out the front door. He also rested just inside the patio door, looking out at the deck, which is surrounded by lovely trees and bordered by a large pond. Brighton had a couple of spots in the house that were especially comfortable for him and near to us. He seemed very content being right in the middle of a room surrounded by the assuring activities of his home and family.

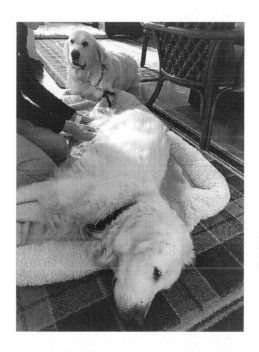

Dr. M. found Brighton to be a delightful patient in the administration of the acupuncture needles. It was obvious that he had total trust in her doing what was good and healing for his body and spirit. Dr. M. would kneel on the floor and use a soothing whisper as she would delicately guide the long, slim acupuncture needles into the various points of Brighton's body.

A few times, Brighton would lift his head to look at us as if to ask, "Are you there? Are you watching?" Then he would peacefully put his head down to embrace the intention of the healing. The process of Dr. M. slowly inserting the needles, plus the peaceful pause for Brighton to absorb the therapeutic calm, would take a total of about thirty minutes. During acupuncture, Pops and I kept the house very quiet to provide him with soothing solitude. I sat nearby on a chair and kept my eyes on Brighton, with Snowdon silent at my feet. Snowdon was very curious and wanted to watch, so he would also sit perfectly quiet and stare at Brighton and Dr. M. Snowdon obviously sensed the peace of this healing therapy, and he remained quieter than usual. He also craved attention from Dr. M. He got a hug from her once the needles were removed, and Brighton was free from his therapy position.

Brighton had visits from Dr. M. twice a week at the onset, and then once weekly, with a slightly longer break over the Thanksgiving holiday. Each time Dr. M. visited, she would carefully and delicately feel the position and size of the tumor located on the spleen. When I would ask her for weekly feedback, her eyes would answer me in a compassionate way and she would say, "The tumor is slowly growing."

By late November, she was starting to respond, "It's big."

It was the week of Thanksgiving when we approached ten weeks since the time of Brighton's initial diagnosis. We were gradually nearing the three-month benchmark that had been his initial prognosis. Now, that timeline was coming to an end.

At the time of his diagnosis, we had prayed with strong hope that Brighton would still be here with us at Thanksgiving. Our family tradition for the Thanksgiving holiday was for the dogs to stay at their favorite paws paradise boarding place while we would fly to Houston to celebrate the holiday at our son's home. In September, when Brighton was diagnosed, we discussed Thanksgiving quite sensitively with our son. We made the realistic projection at that time that we would be unable to travel to Houston for Thanksgiving. Brighton would either be in the final stages of his life or perhaps already would have passed at the time of the holiday.

We considered ourselves very blessed that Brighton was still with us for Thanksgiving. We lovingly celebrated holiday time with our small nuclear family of Pops, Doc, Brighton and Snowdon. Pops always loved Thanksgiving dinner with our son, yet he understood the need to cancel our traditional Thanksgiving in Houston. Instead, Pops made a reservation for the two of us to leave home for a short Thanksgiving dinner buffet at a lovely local restaurant.

Once Thanksgiving was over, Dr. M. returned for a few more acupuncture visits. We began to see subtle signs that the end was creeping up on Brighton. Dr. M. continued to report that the tumor was slowly getting larger. We did not have any signs of an impending rupture, although we were aware that it could happen at any time. We did have the Yunnan Baiyao and the emergency little red pill on hand, which would be used in case of a sudden rupture and severe bleed.

By December 5, we had reached the date that was exactly three months from his initial diagnosis on September 5. Brighton had survived the projected three-month prognosis. That date was on a Thursday, with a visit from Dr. M. Yet, that week Brighton was sinking into a deeper lethargy with significant difficulty getting up.

On Friday, December 6, we were scheduled to attend an especially important Christmas party being held by two of our closest friends at a restaurant that was two blocks from our home. These friends were extremely fond of Brighton, and they had lost their angel, Benson, three years before. They knew what we were going through and, in fact, were lovingly giving us their intuition that we were now near the end. Pops went to the party for a couple of hours, and I stayed home with Brighton. During the time

Pops was gone, I dealt with a diarrhea situation and clean-up that was a definitive clue time was running out. I was right where I belonged with my sweet angel Brighton.

We had reached the end of three months of hospice. During the first half of that time, I had been supported by the hope and prayers that God might bless Brighton with the grace of more days than projected. I did everything I could to give him the energy of healing. Every day for that three-month period, I had spent at least an hour with Brighton resting right in front of me on his comfy bed. Throughout the day, I would make time to just stroke his head and body with pure love. His fur was always so beautiful, and to this day I get tears at the thought of his soft white coat. I loved his legs and paws and his gorgeous horse-like tail. I also especially loved his exquisite long ears and the soft feel of ermine on the top of his head. I cherished everything that was Brighton for every present moment.

The word *hospice* has the word hope woven within it, and every caress of my angel, Brighton, was my prayer of anointment in the hope of healing. Yet, we almost lost Brighton in October with the terrible diarrhea from the Chinese herbs. My hope had gradually faded into faith. Hope somehow meant that I was injecting prayer and energy toward a miracle improvement in his outcome.

I gradually had to accept the wisdom to discard hope and replace it with faith. I now embraced faith that all was in God's hands, and my hands were delivering an angelic tactile message to Brighton. I lived now in the faith that God and Brighton would join hands in the Sistine Chapel of our home at a time that was not mine to alter. Life was now the trinity of hope, faith, and love, living with each present moment in time being carved within the spirit of divine destiny.

SNOW DRIFT (Drifting in time and space)

I would always love visitors to our house, whether it was a delivery person, plumber, or another repair worker. One day, this beautiful lady entered our house.

"Wow! Oh boy, oh boy! Now this is real excitement!" I said. "Plus, she smells like dogs and is obviously here to visit me and Brighton! I've got to jump up and hug her!"

Pops or Doc would hold my wiggling collar and put on my leash to hold me back. In her first visits, Brighton would get up, come near the door, and bark his message of welcome. It quickly became apparent that the visitor was there especially for Brighton, although she also made the polite effort to give me equal attention. I quickly was told the deal: "This lovely lady is actually Dr. M., a vet doctor! Really! The bag she carries is filled with all kinds of doctor stuff!"

When Dr. M. arrives, Brighton would rather go to his comfy bed on the floor of the border between the foyer and the living room. That became his meeting place for Dr. M.'s fun visits. At first, Pops would pull me into the other room while Brighton had his needle treatment. Then I learned to behave so quietly that Doc would let me sit right beside her and Brighton, so I could curiously watch the needle magic.

The visits from Dr. M. started during nice fall weather. Then winter started to get cold and darker. Coats and hats and gloves became a big deal for Brighton and me to go for our walks, which became shorter as time went on. Finally, we had a couple of really weird days. We actually had a *lot* of *snow.* (Hmmm. My name has *snow* in it, so I am sometimes called "Snow.")

During two visits, Dr. M. came into the foyer stamping

her boots. Everyone exclaimed how shocked they were with snow this early! Doc needed a lot of help from Pops, as she had to put the rubber "bootsies" on our feet to take us out for our walk! We seemed in our home to be drifting into winter in a snowdrift! That also seemed to be the way the life at our home was becoming. It was a slow drifting of time. We were all quietly doing our own thing, while watching out for Brighton and staying peaceful. It seemed that there had become little left to say.

I learned during the three months of fall how to be less of a pesky clown. I could not wrestle with Brighton anymore. I could tell they would watch me after eating to be sure I would not playfully try to hump Brighton's rear end. Everyone was treating Brighton with care, and I would hear comments about being careful with his tummy. Ever since I was a pup, I was the goofball that would act like a punk! Brighton would watch me, sometimes in annoyance, and sometimes in fun—or at least built-in entertainment.

I admit that I fell in love with Dr. M. and her visits. I would behave soooo well and quiet. I wanted so much to sit beside Doc and Brighton and watch the weird procedure of slowly pushing long needles into Brighton's skin. I could tell that Pops couldn't even watch. He worked on his computer for several hours every day and watched Dr. M.'s visit out of the corner of his eye. He listened to every word, though; he would often suddenly comment on something Dr. M. would say.

I would sit quietly while thinking to myself, "Oh, I'm so curious about this! I do know about everything that is going on. I get it! I've learned to wait my turn. I'll just give a soft little whine so they don't forget I'm waiting. I'm so anxious to get my hug from Dr. M. Aha! Finally! She's putting her needles away. Here I am! Look at me with open arms and my big drooling smile. Oh boy, oh boy! She has the best hugs and best doggie smells. I can tell how much she loves doggies."

SONG INSPIRATION

"Endless Love" (Lionel Richie duet with Diana Ross)

My love is so strong that my heart feels forever intertwined with Brighton's. The song "Endless Love" is a comforting reminder of the bonds of endless love. The song begins with the expression of only one in life, which can often be the feeling one has with a dog.

The passage to the rainbow bridge is a tenuous step-by-step journey, wearing shoes of dread laced with realization and acceptance that there is an end coming. It makes every moment of each day a precious memory carved into our cellular souls. Yet, their last breath is not the end to that profound divine love that has been infused into our hearts. With each decision, each gesture of care, and each caress, the neurological mystery of the human body registers a miniscule moment of memory that is felt forever. The depth of love for our fur angels creates an endless sense of being, drawn to a desperate yearning that continues to permeate the soul of everlasting life.

5

- -

Good Boy, Goodbye

Surviving the original prognosis was our guiding benchmark. After three months, Brighton walked very slowly around the block, and it was a big celebration of "good boy," every time he walked along with us. He always had the most charming way of stepping with his feet, reminding us of a model delicately walking down a catwalk.

Dr. M. had visited Brighton on Thursday, December 5, the three-month anniversary of his diagnosis. She gave him an acupuncture treatment and reported, "As I palpate, I can tell there's an increased expansion of the tumor on the spleen." She leaned toward me and, with a serious look, whispered, "It's big."

Brighton's energy level and ability to move was increasingly compromised. The appointment on Thursday was the last acupuncture visit from Dr. M. We carefully reviewed what I would do if, and more probably when, over the coming weekend, I might need to use the emergency syringe medication that contained a tranquilizer and pain killer. We reviewed the previous instructions and coaching session, and I felt as ready as I could be for an almost inevitable emergency. I was very scared to use the syringe, but she had me hold it and practice the movement.

The following day was Friday, and Pops left in the early evening for the special Christmas party that was held only five minutes from our home. Our dear friends, who had dealt with the passing of their angel, Benson, were hosting the large holiday event at a local restaurant and understood why I could not leave Brighton in order to attend.

Pops saw that things were quiet and hesitantly said, "I'm sorry you can't go, and I know they understand. Are you sure you will be okay? I'll have dinner there and leave right after. I should be gone less than two hours."

I encouraged Pops to go, assuring him that things would be fine with me there. Brighton had been lying totally flat on his side in our family room and sleeping. I was resting quietly beside him on the ottoman. Suddenly, he started making a sound that indicated he was having some trouble breathing. He needed to be propped up. I tried to lift him off the floor into a position lying on his stomach with his head off the floor, but he was dead weight!

Clever problem-solving was suddenly in order! I needed to think of what to do all by myself to provide Brighton with a better upright position. I thought that if I could move him into the living room, I could prop him up against the couch. I began a responsive plan. I went upstairs and retrieved a large tubular body pillow that was in the shape of a huge U, with about four feet on each side. I dragged it down the stairs, also grabbing and tugging at a small, comfy throw rug from the upstairs hallway. It was ironic that the throw rug was one I had bought years before. It had one large white dog on a dark blue background with a star in one corner and the moon in the other. Back in the living room, I positioned the dog rug on the floor area in front of the couch. Then I propped up the U-shaped body pillow along the long front edge of the couch and laid a quilt over the rug followed by a large towel.

I was impulsively reacting with an action plan to move Brighton while I was alone. All our floors are hardwood, so my next step was to clear away all the other rugs and create a smooth hardwood pathway to slide Brighton out of the family room. I would need to move him five feet out of the family room, eight feet down the central foyer, and then twelve feet past the dining room table adjoining the living room. Then, I would turn him sideways to slide him along the front edge of the couch. Luckily, Brighton was on his dog bed plus a large towel, so his whole body was resting on a movable base. He was lying still and softly breathing but with labor. It was not a severe crisis situation, but it was a slow, creeping drop in any body energy. Taking short pulls of one to two feet at a time, I slid Brighton along the hardwood floors, pulling my cradled angel through his beloved home.

Whew! After about ten minutes, I had positioned Brighton lengthwise along the front of the couch. My next effort was to pull up on the towel from the part bordering his spine and gradually keep tugging and tipping his body weight from a side resting position to a forward turn, where he was being sprawled on his stomach. Finally, he was resting on his tummy with his front legs spread out in front of him. I then went to retrieve a foam pillow that I could use to prop under his chin. My effort to adjust his position was the right thing to do! He was now resting without labored breathing and softly falling into a deep sleep.

During the next hour, Brighton relaxed and unconsciously released some stool. I retrieved some puppy pads, disinfectant wipes, and a pan with shampoo in the water to gracefully clean him while he was resting. Luckily, out on the dining table, I had set all possible supplies I might need for any emergency or unexpected clean-up.

It was hard to believe that Pops had been away at the party for only a period of about two hours. When he returned home, he found things quiet. However, there was an entirely new hospice setup that had been relocated from the family room to the floor bordering the couch in the middle of our living room.

Pops asked, "What happened? How did Brighton get there? Is he okay? I was only gone a short time. Everyone at the party was asking about you."

"Soon after you left, Brighton started making a noise where he was having trouble breathing," I explained. "I freaked out and was scared he might be dying! I knew he needed to be set upright to clear his breathing passages. I was able to slide him through the house to set him here in the living room, propped against the couch. It is better for him to be sitting up."

Pops finally saw that all was quiet and went up to bed. I positioned myself flat on our long leather ottoman, resting face down with my right hand gently stroking my sweet angel. Brighton spent a quiet night sleeping, and it was blessing that he was now on his tummy rather than the former side position.

By Saturday morning, it was becoming apparent that Brighton was slowly and peacefully transitioning into his final time. Since he was on his tummy on a large towel, we were able to pull him to his favorite spot right in the foyer, facing our open front door. He could now look outside, which he so loved to do, and he spent the morning there awake and asleep, resting in repose. By now, I could barely get him to even taste his favorite pumpkin or chicken, and, at best, he was quite thirsty, taking water from the plastic nozzle of a sports water bottle.

Every morning, I had the ritual of walking the dogs early, and they would come back to eagerly pounce on their breakfast that Pops had prepared while we were gone. Pops would always ask for a report as to whether they had pooped, and, if so, it was considered a great way to start the dogs' day! After the dogs were fed and settled down, Pops would need quiet to concentrate on his daily global update on the computer. While Pops was working on the computer, I would normally drive a few blocks to a popular coffee place.

This Saturday morning was also peaceful. Snowdon had gone with me on his walk, and Brighton stayed settled in the foyer and asleep. I then left for about forty-five minutes to have my morning coffee in the car, trying to center and calm myself. It was rather like visiting a very sick person in the hospital and taking a short break from the tension. I was deeply in the process of integrating the dreaded emotionally draining passage. I knew I would be called to remain strong.

While sitting in the car, for some reason, I turned on the radio. Normally, I would listen to my playlist of songs from my phone. For some strange reason, a song came on the radio that was truly a synchronistic message from the divine. The song was "See Me, Feel Me," sung by The Who, from the musical *Tommy*. I listened closely to the song and was struck with the shock of divine grace in an overwhelming message. The lyrics that slowly permeated my being seemed to be a divine directive to lay my hands on Brighton!

"That's it!" I exclaimed to myself in the car.

I could sense the powerful message in the words of the song. Right away, when the song was over, I looked it up again on YouTube and found a version with the lyrics and a video. I played that version on my phone loudly through the car radio several times. I knew that I needed to put my hands on Brighton and softly caress him with my love! Perhaps it could transmit a miracle to him and inspire a rally! It was definitely divine intuition for what I must do. As I returned home, I kept listening to the song blaring, while entering the front door with Brighton in the foyer. I knelt beside him and played the song several times while petting him and singing the words with my intention of inspiring a rally. As if it were God's will, I kept singing the song, over and over and over.

The lyrics permeated the entire spirit of the morning. After playing the song loudly several times with Brighton, I realized it was time for Snowdon's next morning walk around the block. I was emotionally overwhelmed with a speechless yet almost robotic dynamic of living one second at a time. The words of the song continued to transmit messages! Brighton continued to rest quietly by the front door. I began walking Snowdon on our usual stroll around the block, holding the phone against my ear, loudly transmitting the song into my soul.

Snowdon and I reached the sidewalk beside the busier street a block from the house. I was walking in a trance, singing the song, and on the brink of tears. At the moment that we reached the main street, a car passed by, made a righthand turn, and stopped along the curb. Two people got out of the car and were waving vigorously! I had no idea who they were, but they started walking toward us. Snowdon started to get very excited! Of all people, they were our two dearest friends who had moved out of town, but who had come back to host the Christmas party that I was not able to attend the night before! As I have mentioned, our two dear friends had lost their own dear golden retriever, Benson, and they were especially fond of Brighton and Snowdon. Pops had explained why I could not attend their party and had to stay home with Brighton. It was an example of synchronicity that our friends were just heading toward the nearby expressway entrance to return home.

I heard Benson's mom call out, "Snowy Snowman! Oh, there's my Snowy Snowman!"

Our friends hugged me as Snowdon joyfully jumped up on his favorite angel friend. I paused and then sadly related, "Brighton is on his final journey. I just left him lying by the front door, looking out, and I'm going right back to sit with him. He is quiet and peaceful."

I knew it was heartbreaking for our friends to try to console me, as they knew I was in the midst of having to deal with my loss, just like they had dealt with the passing of their angel Benson. This was one of several synchronistic things that had been happening throughout these final days, and I was recognizing each as a message of grace and divine love.

By the time I returned home from the walk with Snowdon, I had sung "See Me, Feel Me" so many times that my whole body, heart, and spirit were all feeling the message of anointing. Anointing, that's what I felt! I knew I had to sit beside Brighton as he rested on the floor looking out the front door. I knew I had to put my hands on him with a gesture to possibly heal, but I was not at all confident that I would be given the gift of healing to be transmitted to him. Obviously, I was feeling a faint sense of hope but also realizing that I had moved beyond hope to faith that what was happening was in God's hands. (How profound is the word *hand*.)

Reality had evolved from hope into faith that the situation was beyond the power of control. It was meant to become Brighton's final divine destiny. I tenuously guided my arms under the towel that was covering Brighton's midsection and gently spread my hands across the surface of his tummy. At the same time, I began to play "See Me, Feel Me" from my cell phone again while softly singing along, making the words my message of prayer. I found my soul sending the message of anointing directly to Brighton's spirit. Of course, I admit I secretly wished my gesture would be given the power to heal him and give him a rally and more time. Nevertheless, at the same time, deep down I also knew it was truly in God's hands, not mine.

After about fifteen minutes of the anointing with touch, I started to pull my arms out from under the towel. As I slid my hands along Brighton's body, I realized that his whole coat was wet where I had been placing my hands! With uncertain confusion, I put my hands back on him and rubbed his fur to confirm the distinct wetness. It was as though he had just finished a deep sweat! I stopped, wondered, and contemplated a profound spiritual conundrum.

Did anointing him with my hands somehow cause Brighton's body to break out in a sweat? Could that be? Did the anointing somehow release a toxic energy inside of him and expel it from his body in heat? I do not know, and I will never know for sure. I only know that I was experiencing a profound moment of merging the physical with the spiritual! I had somehow truly anointed Brighton, perhaps in healing, or perhaps in permission to release and transition. Time would tell. God will tell.

That Saturday was a peaceful, sunny December day for Brighton, resting in his favorite spot and looking out the front door. On and off I would sit beside him on the floor and bring Snowdon over to also spend peaceful family time. We knew this was approaching the unknown moment preceding the end. That night, we slid Brighton back into the living room to his comfortable position alongside the couch, where I had positioned him the night before.

Now my thought was, *Where will be his final resting place in his home on earth?*

It seemed like right in the middle of our living room was the place he was destined to be. I was so relieved that we had an arrangement set for Dr. M. to come to our home for euthanasia. We did not have to anticipate trying to lift him and transport him to the vet when the time would soon arrive. I spent another night sleeping beside Brighton on the long ottoman. By Sunday morning, Brighton had stopped eating and was mostly resting. He did not seem in distress, but he was obviously slipping. I had been watching carefully for the last twenty-four hours to see if there would be any miracle rally, yet the signs were clear. Perhaps the miracle was that he was having a slow, peaceful release, not a rebound.

During Sunday morning I had exchanged several text messages with Dr. M. We agreed that Brighton's end was nearing, and without eating and his gradual slipping, it seemed the time had come for Brighton's rainbow bridge transition at the hands of a loving and caring vet. Dr. M. had an opening for an appointment at nine o'clock on Monday morning, and that became the dreaded rainbow bridge euthanasia moment we knew for three months had been approaching.

All day Sunday, Brighton slept in his final resting place right in the middle of our living room. I would alternate between sitting on the couch and lying on the long ottoman, stroking his body and continuing to transmit my love, softly whispering, "I love you, Brighton. I love you Brighton."

When there were breaks, I would give Snowdon attention. Sitting on the couch with Snowdon, I would attempt to comfort him with some level of understanding and compassion. "It's okay, Snowy. Brighton's our boy."

I have a touching photo of Snowdon resting on the couch, looking at his buddy. At times, Pops would walk into the foyer, not knowing what to say. He spent most of the day in the family room, trying to keep busy at the computer. There was nothing left to say, except Brighton's famous lifelong slogan, "Good boy."

Throughout the day, I kept touching base with Dr. M by text. "Brighton is resting quietly. He doesn't seem to be in pain. Please tell me again what to do with the syringe if he begins to show any sign of distress. I just have to insert the needle into a fold in the skin? I have the syringe kit right here on the table. I understand that the medicine in the syringe includes a prescription tranquilizer and a narcotic pain killer."

This was my last day with Brighton. It was also December 8, a holy day, the feast of the Immaculate Conception. It had always been a special day to me since I was a little girl. In my mind I preferred not to have him pass on that day. For some reason I wanted that day to keep its special Blessed Mother holy day status in my memory. Perhaps, unknowingly, that day was symbolic for me. It was the hardest day of motherhood in my life. I was spending holy time with my baby Brighton. He was sensing me there as his mommy, being with him fully during his final journey toward heavenly passage. I think of it now as being my day to be in synergy with the Blessed Mother. It reminded me of the image of the Virgin Mother Mary also being there with her son, Jesus, during the final hours of His passage through this life.

At around ten in the evening that Sunday night, Brighton began to breathe more heavily. I sensed it was what would be described as more labored breathing. I became anxious and again texted Dr. M. It seemed this was a time to relieve his distress with use of the emergency injection. I became so nervous about administering the injection, even though the instructions I had been given were quite simple. I begged for Pops to sit right next to me and to hold Brighton's head.

"Oh, I'm so nervous, even though I was shown what to do, Pops! I'm supposed to pinch a clump of his fur and skin in the rear of his neck by the base of his skull. Okay, I've got it! Then I just very slowly push the needle into the skin. Okay! Oh! Then slowly press the injection button of the syringe. I'm doing it! Then watch the medicine enter below the skin. I did it! Oh! It wasn't difficult, but I'm so wiped out, Pops!"

Emotionally, it was so profound. Pops helped me rest Brighton's head on the foam pillow that supported his chin. Within ten minutes of the injection, Brighton fell into a quiet, restful sleep and was obviously out of pain. Pops and I looked at each other and had no words to express the fragile moment. It was an exchange of sad silence. We expected Brighton's sedated and painless situation to last into the night. Pops reflected that it was past his usual time for bed, and. I assured him that it was okay.

"You can go upstairs and get some sleep. I'm sure I'll be okay with my baby throughout the night. All is peaceful. I know this is Brighton's final night, and we need to be ready for Dr. M. to be here in the morning."

I often recall how I felt at that time. It was definitely a mature resignation of what I had been bracing myself for my whole life. I knew it was finally meant to be. I felt a need for my love for Brighton to sustain me and pour out to him, and it did. I could not plead with him not to go. In my deep and final motherly love, I had to convey unselfish permission for him to embark on his heavenly journey.

At around midnight, I took about half an hour to busy myself around the house. I would tiptoe quietly from place to place as I made ready for anything that I might need for Dr. M.'s appointment in the morning. I had gone through the motions of setting on the dining table anything I might need for a sudden emergency. I knew I might need wipes, paper towels, puddle pads, ice, water, or first aid supplies. I had no knowledge of whether there might be severe pain, tumor, spleen rupture, or anything else that I might have read or heard might accompany death. The hardest thing about the concept of this type of first aid was that it was no longer to save his life but only to provide love and comfort during the transition of passing.

Finally, with everything in place, I noticed that Brighton's tranquilizer and pain killer medicine seemed to be wearing off. I felt disturbed that his breathing seemed to be getting more restless. I was by myself and watching him with my own quiet distress, frozen in thought of what to do. It occurred to me that, of course, there would be no danger in administering another dose of the syringe. The package that Dr. M. had prescribed contained an original supply of half a dozen fully prepared syringes. So, in the mindset of a caring nurse, I went over and bravely repeated the second injection on my own. Whew! I had administered a new dose of the medicine!

Again, within ten minutes, Brighton's labored breathing subsided, and he fell into a deep sleep. He was lying right beside the long ottoman. Several times throughout that day and night I had reclined on the ottoman, while slowly and lovingly petting him and telling him how much I loved him. How many times can you keep saying, "I love you"? They know you do and have felt and heard it endless times. The love is just so profound and deep!

It was now after midnight, and I was lying on my stomach on the ottoman once again. I had for several hours just petted and caressed and comforted Brighton and loved him once more with every tearful touch. I cherished every stroke of his beautiful fur and every gentle pulsation of his breath. My gentle anointing also gave him permission to let destiny take its course.

Finally, around two in the morning, I became so sleepy that my eyes involuntarily closed. It had probably been an hour that I had been sleeping with my hands on Brighton, when I slowly awoke. I didn't move but felt my hands under his blanket continuing to caress him. I thought to myself, *He is so peaceful!*

Boy, that medicine really has made him relax. I'm glad he's resting so peacefully.

After several minutes, I began to realize that I was pressing to feel his tummy go up and down ever so slightly, yet I could not feel the slightest soft breath. I was lying there perfectly quiet, thinking more and more. *Could he have passed? No!*

The books I had read all said that passing quietly on their own is what we all would wish. Yet it is not very common. The medicine must really have done its work. Slowly and curiously, I then let my hands slip along Brighton's beautiful body. There was a total stillness of warm peace. My hands moved upward to his head and felt what seemed like a delicate, exquisite angel. No breath! No movement! It was a purity of stillness … and peace.

My astounded soul exclaimed, "Oh my God! Brighton is gone! Bless his angel soul. My beautiful boy peacefully snuck out on me. He ascended over the rainbow bridge while I was sleeping. He saved his mommy the pain of watching him leave. He avoided the mutual sadness of parting for the last time in dreaded disconnect from someone of such love. My sweet Brighton left on his own terms. Even in the end, Brighton was a Good Boy. He was the best!"

SNOW STORM

Things were not right in our house. Brighton was resting most of the time. I was not getting extra treats with Brighton, as he strangely did not want to eat anymore. Now, that was really strange! I sensed a lot of extra attention was being given to Brighton. Doc would pet him for hours at a time. She would rest on the big ottoman beside Brighton, with her hands hanging down, stroking his fur. I would quietly go over and lie down to the side of the ottoman right next to Brighton. Then one of Doc's hands would pet Brighton, and the other would equally pet me.

Since Brighton was free during the night, I could see it was best for me not to bother him. I would be snuggled away for the night in my very large, steel wired crate.

I would think, *My big crate is like my doghouse. I actually like it there! When I go in, Pops always gives me treats! It is also the place where my food bowl is placed and where I get my yummy meals!*

Doc or Pops would still take me for strolls and sniffing excursions around the block. For several days, Brighton was no longer joining me for our usual walks. He napped a lot and spent a whole day resting covered with a blanket in the hallway, looking out the front door.

On one afternoon walk, Doc and I were around the block beside the busy street. I was doing my usual sniffing along the way, when I heard some yelling. I looked up and saw two people waving and coming toward us! Oh boy! It was my very best human lady friend who I totally love and adore! I get so excited whenever I see her and her man. I had not seen them in quite a while and really missed them. There they were! They stopped and petted and hugged me in a big reunion.

"Oh Snowy, my Snowy Snowman!" she said.

I was in heaven! Then they talked in a not-so-excited way with Doc. They gave us super big hugs and left to go back to their car. Doc and I walked home. I was sniffing again, and Doc was walking along, listening to music on her phone and softly singing.

Pops was very quiet those days. He finally took me out for my last evening walk down the street.

That last night with Brighton, he was lying very still on a blanket on the living room floor, and I jumped up and rested on the couch above him. All attention for the whole evening was focused on Brighton, and I could tell something serious was going on. There was no laughter, and there was little movement in the house.

About an hour later I was guided into my crate in the family room with treats, and I knew it was time for me to settle down for the night. I am a very good sleeper, yet at times I will look totally sound asleep, but then pop up curiously at any noise. That was the case a few times during the night, as I heard Doc's quiet movement up the stairs and a couple of short phone calls. I closed my eyes and rested as whatever was going on was not a signal for me to awaken.

SONG INSPIRATION

"See Me, Feel Me" (by The Who, from the musical *Tommy*)

The amazing synchronicity of the song "See Me, Feel Me" was a profound grace that blessed me unexpectedly in the final days of Brighton's life. I heard the song quite as a coincidence on the car radio, and I immediately felt throughout my soul that the song was a message for me to place my hands on Brighton and anoint him. I have listened to this song over and over and watch the video on YouTube. It is truly a message that reaches the grief that engulfs the soul in dealing with the heartache of emotions in losing a beloved pet.

The song has a profound message of the emotional power to be found in listening to music. The major message is one of anointing expressed in the words *see, feel, touch,* and *heal,* and the generating of heat. I have always had a passion for mountains, and the song has a metaphor of climbing the mountain. Also, the lyrics can be seen as connecting with death and resurrection in the inspiration of the vision of glory. Likewise, the end of the song reflects on getting the story from "you," and that seems to represent divine Inspiration from God.

6

Phoenix Arising

Brighton was gone! What was I to do? It was about two forty-five in the morning when I found myself lying on the living room ottoman with Brighton's body on the floor beside me. My hands were gently resting on my boy in a final anointing. I was softly stunned and stayed in the same position for perhaps an hour.

Finally, I realized that I should alert Pops, who was sleeping upstairs. I slowly pulled myself upright on the ottoman and carefully peeled myself away from my position beside Brighton. There was a sense of profound reverence that left me speechless and numb, being in the room with my boy who had transitioned peacefully across the rainbow bridge. It was a surreal atmosphere. It was not frightening, not traumatizing, just profound. I think the psyche must enter a state of serene shock to cope with the realization of being in the presence of death. Again, it was not scary but rather manifested in existential reverence.

Every move I made in the middle of that daunting night was slow and peaceful and delicately robotic. I tiptoed upstairs and entered our master bedroom, where Pops was soundly asleep. Quietly sitting on the edge of the bed, I waited in uncertainty. Pops sensed my presence and slowly opened his eyes from a deep sleep. He lifted his head and looked at me with a puzzled expression.

I turned my face toward him, but then had to turn away. I softly said, "He's gone."

The surreal silence that followed said it all. Pops and I were both stunned with profound reverence that our boy had passed on his own terms. We knew that the possibility of a peaceful individual passing was certainly the preference over euthanasia. Yet, it is not often the case and should not be expected. Brighton's gentle, unexpected passage was what we wished for over Dr. M. coming in the morning to put him to sleep. We realized the peaceful way Brighton had flown with his own angel wings. Pops and I were in awe of the beautiful soul of our sweet boy. There were no words that were spoken, as we both were immobile in stunned reverence.

Neither Pops nor I cried at that point in the middle of the night. One could hear a pin drop. We embraced as a mom and a dad honoring profound reverence as though we had experienced an apparition of an angel among us. Being in the middle of the night, there was no need for Pops to get up and disturb the spirit of serenity that had enveloped our home.

Pops was in quiet reflection at this point, yet he knew he had to say something to me. Finally, he whispered, "What time is it?"

I slowly mumbled, "It's after four a.m. I fell asleep around two and then woke up at three. I had my hands on him and began to realize he was gone. I've been staying right there with him, not knowing what else to do."

Pops was obviously stunned and uncomfortable. Finally, in his calm, manly voice, he said, "I'll be down in a while."

I hesitated and then responded, "I'll go back downstairs and stay with Brighton until morning."

I slowly tiptoed down the stairs and sat on the love seat in the family room. Snowdon was in his large crate in the corner of the room. As I look back, it was amazing that Snowdon stayed so quiet. It was almost as if he knew. Finally, I stood up in the foyer, looking at the peaceful scene with my rainbow bridge angel.

I sighed to myself, "Now what do I do?"

I had two dear golden retriever friends who had been with me every step along Brighton's final journey. Both had been in contact with me by texts throughout the day. So, I texted each of them and typed, "Brighton's gone."

It was still the middle of the night, and yet both of my dear friends responded right away with messages of comfort and support. Through text and a short phone call, both immediately wanted to be sure I was okay.

I told them, "I can't believe how profound it is that Brighton peacefully left while I had fallen asleep for an hour, with my hands right on him."

Brighton had always had the image of an old soul and Yoda. He had been true to his B-RIGHT-ON spirit and had wisely slipped across the rainbow bridge on his own. It was a perfectly graceful exit. It was amazing how Brighton totally passed on his own terms, and rightfully so!

It was still the wee hours of morning, and I had about three hours by myself with Brighton's body. It was a final gift of time for me. I went back to stretch out along the ottoman and again stroke him with divine love and reverence. I was choked with tears, but too stunned to sob. I was awestruck with how beautifully Brighton had taken over to accomplish his final B-RIGHT-ON. He had saved me the anguish of having to make the morning decision to put him to sleep. He had snuck out without feeling my anguish in having to watch his final moment of passing. Together, we had been immersed in the union of spiritual peace, softly in touch with each other. Both of us had been sleeping in a quiet middle-of-the-night grace. God chose that moment to physically separate us, which mystically sealed our spiritual bond forever. A part of me had also stepped across the threshold of the rainbow bridge with him.

Snowdon slept that night in his large crate in the corner of the family room. At his usual early hour that morning, he became restless and curious as to what had happened in the living room. I had set up a divider in the foyer, so Snowdon would not be able to immediately rush into the living room and see Brighton.

Again, there is no practice for this type of situation. I did not know what to do. Snowdon stood at the barrier to the living room and seemed to express a soft whine of anxiety and curiosity. Acting solely on intuition, I went over the barricade to Snowdon and softly hugged him. Every word I was speaking was in slow motion and in such a soft, reverent manner. I slipped open a space in the barricade and took a gentle hold of Snowdon's collar. I guided Snowdon over to see Brighton's body. Snowdon quietly approached and smelled Brighton's head, pausing for a long moment to glance at the stillness of the peaceful body of his sweet brother. Snowdon seemed to have integrated enough and then began to turn in readiness to retreat to his more familiar foyer area. It seemed to be a wise decision for me to let Snowdon fully see and smell that Brighton had passed. I then took the time to embrace Snowdon with the same soft touch I had been using with Brighton.

Pops came down the stairs in the morning. I explained that I had decided to give Snowdon the opportunity to fully view what had happened to Brighton. I also realized that this moment was extremely hard for Pops. He also needed time and space to approach Brighton and reverently integrate the reality that his "beggar man" was gone. Facing a body soon after death can be an extremely shocking experience. I realized that it is important to allow everyone to assimilate this delicate circumstance in his or her own personal way. Everyone handles it a little differently, and no one knows until it happens how he or she will respond. Every reaction deserves to be honored. At this point, Pops and I stood in the living room and stared. We then hugged, looking in awe at the angel who had lived within our home and hearts. Brighton was an amazing boy, an old soul who had blessed our lives.

With the sunrise that morning, I reconnected a second time with my two dear friends, who had been through their own death experiences with their golden angels. They had been there, consoling and coaching me along the final journey. I also sent a text message to Dr. M., who had been scheduled to arrive at nine o'clock for her appointment to administer euthanasia. We talked on the phone, and she confirmed that she would still come at the scheduled time. I was grateful that she would be there to support us and could verify for me what had happened in the process of Brighton's peaceful passing during the night. She also offered to call the cemetery to alert them that Brighton would be coming. We would decide whether we or Dr. M. would transport him once she arrived.

What overcame me during this time of mourning was my inner drive to dedicate myself to every minute, every part of the final-resting-place process. I found I did not want Brighton out of my sight, and I was compelled to protect and honor his beautiful body. When Dr. M. arrived, she completed a final examination, verified what had happened, and helped with any vet insurance and cemetery paperwork. She said that, as part of her euthanasia service, she often transports the body.

There is a beautiful pet cemetery located a few miles from our home, and it has a rather famous reputation for its exquisite dedication to the memory of cherished pets. The Hinsdale Pet Cemetery is in a quiet suburban area, and the property is filled with large older trees that have been there since the early 1900s. They have a main building like a small funeral home that contains a very professional facility for cremation, which is used for final arrangements by veterinary hospitals throughout the Chicagoland area.

It was finally time to take Brighton away from our home. I felt a strong need to not say goodbye to Brighton's body by having Dr. M. take him away. Dr. M. had a portable stretcher in her van. We enclosed Brighton in a blanket that was put under his dog bed and then wrapped around him. Dr. M. and Pops slowly and respectfully used the stretcher to carry Brighton's body out to the back of our SUV. It just felt right that we would drive him to the cemetery. Dr. M. had alerted them that we would be arriving.

As we were reaching this next stage of Brighton's final journey, we also had to consider the best arrangement for Snowdon.

I said to Pops, "We can't leave Snowdon alone while we go to the cemetery. He'll be very confused and upset. It wouldn't be fair for him to feel abandoned at home at this time. While you drive the SUV, I'll sit in the back seat holding Snowdon to keep him still while Brighton is in the hatch area."

Pops nodded in agreement, as he was feeling the uncertainty of the situation both for himself and Snowdon. Really, in hindsight, it was only fitting as a family that we all escort Brighton to the cemetery. By now, we were all operating in a quiet, stunned, respectful loyalty to our angel.

When we arrived at the pet cemetery, the people could not have been more supportive and compassionate. They brought out a wheeled stainless steel medical table to take Brighton into the reception area. We were asked if we would still like to have more time with our boy, and we said yes. So, they took Brighton in the back area to help prepare him for us, while we went into an office to sign papers verifying final directives and payment for cremation.

This very professional pet cemetery and cremation facility has a legacy history in the Chicago area dating back over fifty years. We were offered the option of a private cremation, and privacy was very important to me. The first opening they had for a private cremation with a private viewing was a week from the day he had died. In the meantime, he would be kept in appropriate frozen containment for the week until cremation. This actually became comforting for me to have a little more time before fully having to emotionally deal with the final disintegration of Brighton's body.

Finally, we were given the opportunity to go back into a lovely little viewing room as soon as the paperwork was complete. By this time, they had placed Brighton in a casket-shaped box, tucked in with his blanket on his bed. Snowdon was still with us during this entire time. While waiting in the lobby area, he had been making friends with a couple of cemetery staff members who could not have been kinder. Now, in this viewing room, I stood next to the casket box with Brighton. Pops stood slightly behind me, holding Snowdon's leash. Snowdon stayed respectfully in a sit position.

It was at this final viewing time that I began to drown in a watershed of tears. I felt such a need for time—more time, more time! We were given as much time as we wanted in the privacy of the viewing room. Pops knew I needed a significant amount of crying time, so he stepped back and sat on a chair, with Snowdon sitting quietly at Pops's side. It made no difference how I looked or how long I took, I just had to sob and sob and sob. I had to touch Brighton for as long as I could for this last time. It was one of Pops's finest moments to understand my anguish and wait without any inclination to encourage me to leave. His silence was truly golden, and so was Snowdon's.

It is these final gestures with a beloved fur angel that truly leave the heart broken and shattered. The moment is so hard and so final. I see how traumatizing it is for any pet owner to say goodbye to their beloved fur angels at the vet hospital and then walk out without them. It is no wonder that such an experience totally leaves the deep scar of a broken heart. How deeply profound is the terrifying moment of goodbye and the unforgettable last touch.

We had a week between the day Brighton died and the day of the scheduled private cremation. That week for us was spent in a fog. Anything related to Brighton was left in its place at home. We gave Snowdon extra time, since he was showing signs of realizing that he no longer had his brother as his constant buddy in the house. Our home life for the last three months had been totally revolving around Brighton. We had almost always had one of us at home out of fear that if we were both gone, Brighton might bark incessantly. Snowdon was used to us surrounding both boys in the first-floor rooms of our house.

Our home sweet home had always had activity that now had been reduced by 50 percent. We felt a reluctance to leave Snowdon totally alone in the house, as he had never been alone before. He had always had Brighton from the time he first arrived as a pup. Snowdon and I were both acting as though a huge void had overcome us, and indeed it had. The loss of Brighton was like a vacuum, sucking the angelic spirit out of our life!

Pops and I had mixed emotions about the upcoming private cremation appointment. The whole week in between had been somewhat comforting for me to realize that Brighton's body was being reverently stored at the cemetery. The morning of the private cremation, we took Snowdon to spend the day at doggie daycare. It was obvious that Snowdon had been struggling with Brighton's loss more than expected, and he needed a recharging break by returning to the playtime of a dog's life.

We arrived for the private cremation appointment about thirty minutes early. After waiting a short time, we were guided into a small viewing room with a large glass picture window that had a curtain, which could be closed to block viewing into another large laboratory-type room. They had brought the casket box with Brighton into our small viewing room. The cemetery staff treated Brighton's body and the feelings of his family with such incredible respect. We were guided into the room and told we could take as much time as we liked to be with Brighton before the cremation would begin. They also left the door open from the small viewing room to the wide hallway outside the door that contained two comfortable tapestry-upholstered chairs where family members could sit and wait.

Pops and I slowly walked in to view Brighton, beautifully and delicately tucked in his casket. I reached out to put my hand on his fur. This was so hard on courageous Pops, and he slowly backed away to sit in one of the chairs outside the room. In silent love, he realized that the emotional, maternal side of me needed a special portion of time to spend my last moments with my precious baby. I stood there with Brighton for probably fifteen minutes. I just kept touching him and sobbing tears that would not stop flowing down my cheeks. The vat of love inside me was bursting with the rupture of a tearful goodbye. Oh, God, it is so sad and so filled with overwhelming anguish!

I knew I finally had to detach from Brighton. As the saying goes, it was time to "let go, and let God." I did one last gesture of anointing by trimming off some fur from Brighton's exquisite English crème coat. Then I removed a few of those most cherished strands from his gorgeous golden tail that I wanted to hold onto forever. I loved that beautiful tail so much and adored his sweet floppy ears. I had so many pictures of his ears, and they were the cutest, framing his beautiful face. Finally, I summoned the courage to use my phone for some last photos. I was grasping for one more moment to see him before he would be gone forever. Oh, the pain was as deep as the love!

After a lengthy decision for cremation over burial, I integrated a tenacious resolve to watch the entire process. The Hinsdale Animal Cemetery had a truly first-class cremation service. They had clearly outlined for me the complete information as to the options in cremation. I immediately knew I wanted a private and personal cremation procedure that was a special time reserved just for Brighton. I also felt, for some reason, that I had to watch the entire cremation process. This was an option offered and honored with respectful accommodations. Some may wonder or be shocked as to why I felt a calling to watch the entire cremation process. I can only say that I felt a profound calling to my deep sense of loyalty and love that is impossible to describe.

The room for the final viewing had a window that looked directly into the very large laboratory-looking room. It held a gleaming steel cremation oven, plus other tables available to neatly organize the process. As I looked at the cremation room through the window, I was comforted by its level of cleanliness and sterile appearance. It was equipped with shiny stainless-steel tables and large gleaming furnace equipment, which gave everything a sense of subsequent order and respect. I had been given a sensitive overview of everything that was to happen. I was welcome to watch the entire process through the window, leave the room for a while, or ask at any point to have the drape drawn over the window.

The moment came when I touched Brighton goodbye for the

last time. I had to acknowledge at that point that he was already gone from life to help me accept the impending process. They rolled his coffin box out of the viewing room and through the door of the cremation room. My eyes suddenly became totally fixed and not blinking for a moment. I felt determined to watch every move that was made to respectfully honor Brighton's body. I had no idea how I would handle this situation. I was only able to follow my heart in an instinctual response of total love and loyalty. I do not want to describe in detail everything I saw. It was not horrible, but only what one would expect in viewing the opening of a furnace or oven. What is more meaningful to me is to share with others the deep, intense devotion I felt to have my eyes stay with him during every second of this final leg of his journey of transition to spirit. I can assure others of the meaningful respect they showed.

With my feet planted at the window of the viewing room, I will always recall how compelled I was to never blink my eyes. I had to be with my Brighton the entire time, to seal our pact of love that is carved eternally in heaven. As the oven door was closed, I kept staring in a profound feeling of the deepest pure love. I was desperately willing my spirit to reach through the window, across the oven room, and into the body I had loved with all my heart and soul. The feeling of shock was not horrible, just so gut-wrenching and profound. I was breathing in a reserve of courage to face this final ritual of devotion.

I realized how much I had always looked after and protected Brighton, and now I was right there protecting his spirit in dedicated motherly love. I suppose it is like a mother who has to escort her child to surgery and finally needs to release the child with love and trust. The mind becomes a heart and never leaves the cherished bond during the entire time of a surgical procedure. I had also had that type of surgical experience with Brighton, and, looking back, perhaps it was that experience of motherly love that fueled me to be with my boy even through the anguish of this profound end.

The cremation process took about an hour and a half. During that time, I never left my spot by the window, and my eyes never left the focus on the huge, gleaming furnace. Most of my time was spent standing, staring, with tears rolling down my face nonstop. In the course of the process, I had set up my phone on the windowsill to be ready to play the song "See Me, Feel Me." I pressed the button to play the song over and over and over, while I softly mouthed the words as my spiritual bonding message with Brighton. The song made the tears flow more intensely, and it was the flood I had been holding inside.

Pops stood near me for a portion of the time and then moved into the hallway to sit and wait in one of the comfortable upholstered chairs. He knew that I needed to sob and pour out my grief without looking away from my steadfast stare of final connection. The song was so meaningful. I would forever have carved in my heart these final moments of seeing, feeling, touching, and healing. Yet, I realized that the healing part was meant to be accomplished by Brighton's move to the other side of the rainbow bridge, where he would be his joyful self forever. It also made me think of the legend of the Phoenix, rising from the ashes. Brighton was rising from the ashes of age, to enjoy everlasting life as his playful angel spirit! Would I also be able to rise from this anguish?

Once the procedure of cremation was complete, I was allowed

to watch every single step involved in transferring the ashes to the precious silver picture cube container that I had carefully chosen as an alternative to a traditional urn. Again, I did not take my eyes off the procedure for one second. I felt fixated on knowing that Brighton's body had been handled with respect and reverence, and it truly was. Again, I realized that what I was watching was more than most would choose to do. I try to rationalize that, as a profoundly passionate person, I had been fixated on staying the entire course.

I can attest that I was a witness to 100 percent evidence that Brighton was being returned to me in the cherished silver receptacle. Perhaps my witness to this total procedure may have been meant to bring a stronger sense of confidence to others as to the deep respect shown throughout the entire cremation process. I had often wondered about cremation, and this was a unique and profound experience to be present as a witness. I had several small urns of ashes at home from several of my bunnies who passed. Yet, in those previous cremations, I had accepted with faith and trust that the ashes of my precious bunnies were truly in the containers. As a witness to Brighton's entire cremation, I am sure that the silver picture cube I had chosen as his final resting place definitely contains my boy. That gives me such comfort and reassurance every time I touch his cube and say, "Good morning, Brighton."

We waited outside the cremation room door. When it opened, a very reverent staff member delicately presented me with the silver photo cube that I knew contained Brighton. He was coming home with us. I had brought a wicker basket with a lovely bow on the handle, and I placed the cube in the basket for the drive home. Before we left, the extremely compassionate cemetery staff extended beautiful gestures of comfort and heartfelt closure that I will never forget. Kindness and respect is such a grace, and it is truly a divine calling to help others through any funeral, burial, or cremation process. Bless all who are involved in such a valuable ministry!

As Pops and I drove home from the cemetery, we reflected on the decision process we had considered between burial in the lovely cemetery we had just left and the cremation we had just experienced. It was mid-December on the day of cremation, and it had been raining and dreary. I think the weather became a sign for us that we had made the right decision in cremation. I held Brighton in the basket on my lap. If we had gone ahead with burial, I don't feel I would have been emotionally able to turn away and leave him buried in the ground at the cemetery. This was especially true in December, where we had already had our first snow, and January was coming with frozen ground and winter cold that lasted until April.

To this day, I can't imagine having my sweet Brighton out there in the cemetery alone and not at home. The ashes in the silver photo cube have become the center of a spirit corner of remembrance in our living room that gives us comfort every day. I greet Brighton every morning when I open the shutters and welcome the brightness of the morning sun. I do feel a sense of relief every day that he is home with us forever.

The Phoenix is a mythical bird from ancient Greek legends. The bird lives for several hundred years before it dies by setting itself on fire. Then it starts a new life from the ashes of the fire. The Phoenix represents transformation, death, and rebirth in its fire. It is a powerful ultimate symbol of strength and renewal The Phoenix animal guide is symbolic of the sun, which dies in setting each night and is reborn in rising the next morning. To rise like a Phoenix from the ashes is to emerge from a catastrophe stronger, smarter, and more powerful.

In this book, Brighton's story of forever spirit takes him to the ashes of his life on earth and his rising as a beautiful forever spirit in our lives.

SNOW MORE

I had gone to sleep in my crate in the family room, after leaving Brighton sleeping on a bed in the middle of the living room. During the night there had been some soft talk and tiptoe sounds several times. In the morning, Doc led me out of my crate quite early. I saw a type of low wall set up between the foyer and the living room. I became very curious, as Doc was staying on the other side of the wall in the living room. I was thinking Brighton must still be there, resting where I had left him the night before. Since I am also very attached to Doc, I began to softly whine, as I sometimes do when I want attention.

When I curiously looked at the barricade in the foyer, Doc opened the fence to allow me into the living room. She held my collar and calmed me with whispers as I anxiously pranced into the guarded space. Then I stopped and looked at Brighton on the floor. He had not moved since the night before. Doc held me, and in a very gentle way led me over so I could smell Brighton. I knew it was a different smell, and Brighton was not moving or breathing. It was puzzling, yet my animal instinct told me Brighton's life was no longer there.

Dogs may not use the word *death*, but we know only too well when there is a body without life. Since the heritage of animals is from the wild, our species and ancestors have more experience with death than humans. Plus, animals do not live nearly as long as human beings. Once I could smell that Brighton's life was gone, I paused for a short time, taking an extra look at him. Then I was okay and returned to wait in the foyer.

Finally, Pops came down, as usual, in the early morning. He took me out for my typical routine: a short walk around the block, and then we returned home so I could quickly dash to my crate for breakfast. The rest of that morning was odd, to say the least. The fence was still set across the open space between the foyer and the living room, with Brighton on the other side.

I heard Doc saying to Pops, "I took Snowdon in to see Brighton, and he's okay. It was the right thing to do. I think he understands."

I had a sense to stay out of the way during that whole quiet time. I rested on the cool marble floor in front of the fireplace near my crate. That is my favorite safety spot, and this was a morning when I felt I needed to be quiet and wait for the next happening of the day. About two hours after I had my morning walk, Dr. M. arrived, and I was so happy to see her! I started to jump up, wanting a hug. Pops pulled me back, and I had the cue that, as in the past, the first attention from Dr. M. was to be given to Brighton. I quietly waited and truly knew the command, "Wait."

Dr. M. was in the living room with Doc and Pops and Brighton for quite a while. Finally, I saw the front door open and stood farther back, watching Dr. M. and Pops carry out a flat kind of bed with Brighton wrapped in his blanket. I was getting very anxious now, and Doc quickly came in from outside and gently hugged me and put on my leash. I walked with Doc slowly to Pops's bigger SUV and was surprised that Pops and Doc were trying to get me into the back seat! Doc sat beside me and held my leash. Pops was driving. I knew Brighton was in the back, where I would usually travel in a dog crate. I was very nervous the entire ride, and Doc worked to calmly hold me still.

After a weird drive in the pouring rain, Pops finally stopped the car, and both he and Doc helped to slowly move me out of the back seat and keep me in a sit command while I watched what was happening. We were in what looked like a huge park with a lot of trees and many rows of large stones. A wheeled table was rolled out, and some people took Brighton into a nice fancy building. Pops let me mark a spot on the grass, and then I knew I had to behave as we walked into the quiet building. Doc was already there, sitting in an office with a lady at the desk who acted excited to see me and gave me a smiling welcome. Again, there was polite wait time, and somehow, I felt very important being allowed to be there and being treated like a family member and not just a dog.

We had to wait outside the office in a nice open room, and some other people stopped to pet me and say how good a boy I was. I liked the way they smiled and said "Hi, Snowdon." Finally, the lady took us into a little room where Doc and Pops acted very quiet and sad. On a table was a big, long box. We stood beside the box, and Doc began to cry. I could not see into it, but somehow I knew Brighton was inside. We all stood next to him for a short time, and then Pops backed me up to sit beside him on a chair outside the room. Pop was just quiet and kept his hand on me. Doc stayed next to Brighton for a long time and cried a lot. I had never seen Doc like that.

When we finally left the big park, we came home to what felt like a very empty house. It was obvious that Brighton was not there anymore. At least I knew where he was and that he had not suddenly disappeared. Doc took me for a longer walk. In fact, all week, Doc took me for longer walks than usual. The house was so empty without Brighton that we all needed to find something to do or else take a nap. I found that I needed to take a snooze more than ever. It seemed the whole house was like Brighton when he was last with us: quiet, barely breathing, in a state of snooze. Our house was not the same. I did not feel the same. I missed Brighton being there. By the end of the week, I felt it had been forever, and sometimes I would whine, missing my dog buddy. I was feeling too alone, even with Doc and Pops there. I didn't like being the only dog and getting all the attention. It wasn't as much fun. Brighton wasn't here anymore.

SONG INSPIRATION

"I've Been This Way Before" (by Neil Diamond)

In transferring the content of this book from my mind to written format, I have been discovering songs that I would play to help me through the grief process. Some songs suddenly cross my path by pure accident. Yet as soon as I hear it, I feel it has an angel message.

I have been a fan of Neil Diamond for years, inspired by the messages that I identify with when listening to his recordings or playing his songs on guitar or piano. I have several Neil Diamond song books. Ironically, I had put on a Neil Diamond CD while I was organizing some books on a shelf. There were several familiar songs on it, but then I heard the song "I've Been This Way Before." It totally enchanted me with lyrics that popped out with tremendous connection and inspiration. I replayed the song, and then played it over and over for days and watched it on YouTube.

I knew this song had a special message for me about Brighton! Key words include *light* and *flame*. *Light* became a key word that connected with Brighton's name. *Flame* was integral to cremation. I feel such love with the verse that expresses seeing the loved one again. A climactic verse really strikes the image that some only see the light in death. Through Brighton, I have seen the light, so bright! This song continues to provide comfort in the saga of grief. Its message is truly enlightening. The image of being released is free and ascending. Plus, the certainty of being this way again is comforting, like the Phoenix rising from the ashes.

7

. . . .

Rainbow Dots

Years ago, Pops and I stayed in an expensive rental home for a week's winter vacation along the seashore. The house had a magnificent master bathroom with crystal knobs on the faucet of the Jacuzzi tub. One morning, it was especially sunny. As I was getting ready in the bathroom, I glanced over at the sun shining through the large window above the tub. I saw the most amazing thing! The beams of sunlight were shining right through the round crystal faucet knobs, creating a beautiful spray of rainbow dots on the surface of the tub spreading down to the floor. I will never forget that amazing apparition of spectral light science, and it was planted in my mind forever. It was a sign that there are invisible things beyond what we can see.

Fast forward at least fifteen years to Brighton's three-month hospice situation. I was dealing with every thought and action that was becoming a memorial moment to treasure Brighton's journey to his final destination. My mind kept thinking about everything related to how I could cope with Brighton's passing. I wanted him to know that I believed he could return to visit me in the spirit of his afterlife.

As I was flipping through channels on TV one day, I came across a home shopping network commercial for the sale of a beautiful Waterford crystal horse. I immediately remembered the rainbow spectrum created years earlier by the crystal faucet knob! I responded to a flash of insight and raced to the internet, entering the terms "crystal golden retriever" or "crystal dog." My first thought was to check the website of Waterford crystal to see if they carried any crystal dogs in addition to horses. The search did not lead to a Waterford dog, but it led me to Swarovski crystal. Swarovski did have a few miniature crystal dogs of adult or puppy size. One adult dog was about three inches high and was listed as a mother Labrador retriever, but as I stared at it, I realized I could also interpret the dog as an adult golden retriever. This Swarovski crystal dog was priced over $100, but I thought it was a perfect piece to "crystalize" a rainbow signal for Brighton. Without hesitation, I bought it, ordering it for quick delivery.

Within two days, the Swarovski crystal dog arrived, beautifully packaged in a classy indigo-blue jewelry case. I delicately unpacked it and held the crystal dog in my hand. It was exquisite and had an exceptional number of facets in the cut of the crystal. I unpacked it on our large table next to the foyer where Brighton would be lying for hours every day. He was resting there at that moment. I immediately got down on the floor to hold the crystal dog right above his front paw so he could look at it. I showed him the crystal dog and, like a little kid, began to give him instructions. "Brighton, see this crystal doggie? This is the signal you will use to keep in touch with me! If I hold the doggie a certain way in the sunlight, the beams will shine through the crystal and make rainbow dots. I'll show you tomorrow and we can practice!"

The following morning there was bright sunlight shining through the large clear glass of our front storm door. Brighton was resting on his bed in the foyer. I looked around and found a square glass vase and set the vase upside down halfway between the door and Brighton. I placed the crystal dog on the downturned vase to give it some height. Then I moved the delicate crystal around on this glass pedestal until it was in a position where the sunlight would be transmitted through its facets. It worked! On the space between the crystal dog and Brighton, there was a spray of rainbow dots that spread on the floor. Like magic, the spectrum flashed outward right to the front part of Brighton's head and paws!

The magic of the rainbow dots that were transmitted through the crystal dog was so inspiring that I repeated the same ritual every morning. At other times during the day, I would show Brighton the rainbow dots when there was bright sunlight beaming into other parts of the house. By the second day, I had made Brighton quite aware of the rainbow dots. I would continue to tell him that it was through the dots he would connect with me. I repeatedly told him and demonstrated the spectral magic so many times, that I felt confident we had integrated the spiritual signal between us for our forever secret rainbow-dot code!

It was the morning after Brighton had died when I sadly set foot into the emptiness of our foyer, with Snowdon at my side. There was such a void in the house. I opened the wooden front door, and bright sun beamed through the glass storm door. I immediately grabbed the crystal dog and placed it in the same spot in the foyer where I had done all the rainbow-dot training with Brighton. Sure enough, a spray of rainbow dots spread across the floor where Brighton would lie! The dots came to rest right on the front of Snowdon's paws and nose! I was stunned with emotion! I felt a profound wave of love combined with loss, and yet I believed that Brighton's spirit was there with us. I didn't feel he had come back, as in my mind he had not left. I knelt on the floor, caressing the rainbow dots on Snowdon, and turned to see how far the spectrum of dots had extended.

Amid the magic moment of the rainbow dots resting on Snowdon and the floor, I had also turned my head further to look into the living room. My eyes were drawn directly to the spot in the middle of the living room floor where Brighton had passed the day before. The dog rug was still in the same place with the large ottoman beside it, where I had slept with Brighton the night he had died. Lo and beyond! There was an extended beam of sunlight that flowed into the living room and was spread across the spot where Brighton had passed, directly over the ottoman where I had slept! The sunlight was being filtered through the plantation shutters in our living room, creating an image of large angel wings. Normally,

I close those shutters every night, but for some reason, that night I had left them open. The morning had welcomed the bright spirit of Brighton back into our home and hearts. I was truly amazed, and felt so blessed with the angel grace that filtered through the creeping sense of loss that was destined to haunt me for months.

With the appearance of the rainbow dots through the crystal dog and the winged sunbeams through the shutters, I became aware of the irony and significance of the "living" room. It would become a hallowed spirit place for us to keep Brighton in our home forever. The far lefthand corner of the living room already had white shelving halfway up the wall to display several large figurines, including my collection of Don Quixote sculptures. (I had always been inspired by the Man of La Mancha song, "The Impossible Dream.") The shelving ironically also held a genuine autographed racing helmet in a clear display case. That helmet could be perceived symbolically as a connection with the message from the film *Racing in the Rain*. Also, above the figurines, there was a beautifully framed professional photograph of Brighton, and around the corner was a similar professional photo of Snowdon. It seems the corner of this "living" room had already been mystically prepared as a lovely type of spirit corner and permanent altar setting to memorialize Brighton.

During the week between Brighton's passing and the cremation, life was suspended within a tangible void filled with memories and signs of Brighton. It was December, and yet every day that week seemed to be sunny. Plus, we had daily rainbow dots projected into our foyer and shining on Snowdon, and then, in a comforting way, also reflecting on my hands. We received several cards of condolence from friends, plus two meaningful memorial picture frames. One had the message, "You were my favorite hello and my hardest goodbye." Another dear friend had a picture frame personally inscribed with "Brighton, 2019." The message on that frame was, "When tomorrow starts without me, don't think we're far apart. For every time you think of me, I am right here inside your heart."

Very dear, lifelong friends in San Francisco sent an email certificate of a star register. It reads, "This certificate proves that the star named Brighton Stone with coordinates RA 2h 12 m 22s, DEC 30 Degrees 18' 13"/. Registration Date" 12.09.2019 CONSTELLATION Triangulum, REGISTRATION NUMBER 9DF4B275E." A beautiful tribute on the certificate reads, "Brighton shined brightly every day he was on earth, so it seems only fitting his heavenly star shines for all eternity." We were also given a portfolio that included a map of the sky so we could locate the star named Brighton Stone. That framed certificate is displayed in prominence in the spirit corner as a tribute to Brighton.

A week after Brighton's death, we had the final arrangement of an extremely profound private cremation. We immediately brought Brighton's ashes home with us. They had been professionally placed in a silver photo cube designed for ashes, with room for photos on three sides, and the fourth side inscribed with Brighton's name and life dates: "Born: 7-4-2006, PEACE: 12-9-2019." The top of the cube was left open so it could be crowned with the Swarovski crystal dog. We had a heavy antique crystal fruit bowl on a pedestal that was an heirloom from Pops's mother, who had died some years before. The cube was given prominence on the top spirit corner shelf by being placed on display in the crystal bowl, with Brighton's collar surrounding the cube. I placed a beautiful, large, heavy glass candle jar inscribed with the University of Notre Dame on the side. It had a strong lid that sealed the container, and it became a perfect receptacle to hold the treasured fur relics of Brighton's coat and tail.

Brighton's private cremation had been on December 15, and we were now very close to Christmas. There was no way to emotionally bring myself to put up our traditional, full-sized elaborate Christmas tree. It usually displayed an extensive collection of over sixty dog ornaments as well as other shiny ornament balls. A couple of years earlier, we had been given a tall, thin table-size gold Christmas tree with lights already built into the branches as an anniversary gift. The lights were the same color as an English crème golden retriever's coat. The year of Brighton's death, I decided to break tradition and avoid the difficult and emotional chore of putting up the large tree. Asking Pops's permission, I made a decision to honor the serenity of this Christmas by using the smaller clear lighted tree. I also went through our dog ornament collection and selected only golden retriever ornaments for this year's serenity Christmas tree. The tree was set on a bench with framed pictures of Brighton resting under the tree. Any gifts would be placed on the floor in front of it on the dog rug that Brighton had been lying on when he passed.

I had not done any Christmas shopping in early December because we were so close to Brighton's passage. Finally, I was quickly trying to purchase a few Christmas gifts for family members at local stores. In shopping at a nearby men's store, I walked past a floral shop, and something in the florist's window immediately caught my eye. There was a window display with a silver bucket that had painted on the side in large red words, "Making spirits bright." I immediately took a speedy detour into the florist shop and was able to purchase the silver bucket with the important word, *bright*, on it. Across the street from the florist was a coffee shop where I regularly stopped. The following morning, I was in line waiting my turn to order coffee, when I saw a display of gift cards on the counter. One card jumped out at me! The message on the gift card holder announced, "All is bright." I immediately bought myself a gift card, and it is still displayed on the spirit corner shelf.

Pops always loved Christmas, and he almost lived as the spirit of Santa Claus every holiday season. That year was somber for our resident Santa Pops. Christmas was also difficult for me, as it was only two weeks after Brighton's passing. It was truly an effort to think of gifts, and I had told Pops I did not really want anything. The only thing I wanted for Christmas was to have Brighton with us, as he had been on Thanksgiving. Yet a Brighton Christmas was not meant to be. There had been many times when others I knew had lost family members or pets. I had purchased a remembrance gift of a beautiful angel figurine by the artist Jim Shore for them. There was an angel I had once seen that I especially liked, but I realized that this angel was meant for me. So, I let my son know that the angel was a Christmas gift I would especially like. I did receive the angel as a special Christmas reminder of Brighton. It is a beautiful, large white angel with a flowing skirt adorned in a snow-white mountain scene. Standing in front of the angel is a large white dog, and the angel has her arm outstretched, holding a large white hawk or dove. The angel was an exquisite image of my angelic bond with Brighton!

As Christmas approached, I needed to create an atmosphere of serenity in our living room. It was our normal center for a large elaborately decorated Christmas tree, yet now the room was being held in delicate respect as the place where Brighton had passed into his angel life. A beautiful spirit corner had blossomed in his remembrance. I still had the "Making spirits bright" silver bucket but needed something appropriate to put into the bucket. Pops was friendly with the local florist. I asked him to stop into the floral shop to see if he could buy some display tree branches that had been painted white.

Dear Pops came home with his arm full of two huge bunches of white branches! One set of branches made a beautiful nature setting when set in the silver bucket and placed on the top shelf of the spirit corner. For the other bunch, I had a glass display vase, and the white branches looked truly exquisite in the vase set on a pedestal on the other side of the room beside the new smaller golden retriever Christmas tree. The white branches created such a beautiful sense of nature's serenity that they have become a permanent part of the evolving decorating scheme of our living room. The spirit corner has also become a place where I now keep a crystal vase of freshly cut white flowers, and I regularly replace them throughout the year. It is a constant memorial bouquet set beside Brighton's silver cube of treasured ashes.

During the holidays I became aware on Facebook of a gifted artist from Wales, in the United Kingdom, who does exquisite portraits of dogs. I contacted the artist to get information about having him create an original portrait of Brighton, and as a result sent a deposit. I told the artist that I would share various photos of Brighton to help decide the best one to use as the model. We went back and forth via email with sample photos of Brighton. Once the plan was finalized, the artist agreed to have Brighton's portrait completed, framed, and shipped so it would be in our hands by Brighton's birthday on July 4.

It was obvious that the artist from Wales had several portrait orders on his reservation list prior to Brighton's, yet I felt a desperate need for a life-sized picture of my angel to dominate the wall above the spirit corner. At this same time, I happened upon a special advertisement that mystically appeared in my email from a company that makes beautiful canvas portraits at various sizes. A special offer for a significant discount attracted me to make an impulsive decision to order a life-sized canvas portrait of Brighton. I would use one of the digital photos I had presented to the artist in Wales in planning this portrait and was able to skillfully crop one of the photos and email the digital photo file with my order.

The significant discount in the special portrait offering actually encouraged me to order two canvases. I selected another picture of Brighton's head and shoulders, with his eyes looking straight ahead at me. It would be a large, 18 x 22-inch framed portrait in a modern silver frame. That was purchased in addition to the full-sized frontal image of Brighton. Again, both portraits had Brighton's eyes looking straight forward at me. This life-size portrait was a huge poster with no frame, and the canvas was wrapped around a frame of one-inch depth. Both canvas portraits arrived within a week, and I was so amazed and comforted by the significance and quality! The poster-sized portrait is actually larger than Brighton was! It makes the most comforting reminder of him as he looks at us every day from his spirit corner while we are watching television. I cannot say enough about how this larger-than-life canvas poster keeps Brighton warmly with us as part of our home and family.

In addition to the spirit corner, there have been other signs that have regularly appeared to me as afterlife messages from Brighton. The bright light spectrum of rainbow dots made me aware of beams of light being a "bright" sign. I found that, in an upstairs guest room, the window is positioned in such a way that on any sunny day, in early afternoon, beams of light shine through the window and rest on a bed along the wall. I often have Snowdon join me up in the guest room, and we can sit on the bed and savor a kiss of sunbeam as a sign from Brighton.

I also take Snowdon out for his morning walk around 6:45 a.m. On any sunny morning, the rising sun at that time is positioned so a lengthy beam of sunlight shines right across the front of our house and lands on the driveway. On our usual walk, again, beams from the rising sun shine on us as we stroll along, and I feel comfortable saying, "Aw, good morning, Brighton! Thank you for the hug." I feel like the shadow created beside me from the sunbeam feels like invisible warmth from Brighton.

As early spring came after a cold and cloudy winter, another surprise visit came from Brighton. I had been reading several books over the winter about pets and the afterlife, and several books described various signs to recognize. One was the appearance of a red cardinal. Sure enough, one morning soon after Brighton's passing, a cardinal sang to us from high on top of a tree! It matched the cardinal sign that I had read in the book. Since the first day the red cardinal sang to us, this symbolic bird has been calling to us every day from high on top of various trees as we take our morning walks around the block. Several times, I have taken a short video of the cardinal chirping and posted it on Facebook. It is so delightful to feel that Brighton is saying hello to us through the singing of the cardinal!

Several afterlife books point out that the red cardinal visits after the loss of a dear pet. In *Signs From Pets in the Afterlife—Identifying*

Messages from Pets in Heaven by Lyn Ragan, she explains the following: "The cardinal's voice is strong and clear and reflects an air of importance. This power-packed bird can teach us how to express our truth, develop confidence, and walk our talk. If we respect its teachings, it will lead us home." Ragan continues, "The red cardinal symbolizes importance and faith. There's no surprise this bird is often chosen as a messenger to deliver a meaningful declaration. One that says ... spirit is with you."[4] It seems the voice of the cardinal is guiding me to write this book!

Besides recognizing many signs that I feel are from Brighton, I developed a very close friendship on Facebook with someone in Louisiana who had direct experience with an animal communicator. I was so excited to find someone who actually knew about this and who could give me a personal recommendation as to the trustworthy credentials of the guide who could connect me with Brighton. I contacted the communicator via email and was able to schedule a phone appointment within a few weeks.

On the day of the animal communicator phone appointment, I had a thirty-minute session where I began telling her a little about Brighton. Then she took my information as a stimulus to make a connection. She related to me what she saw and heard from Brighton. "Yes, I see him being very happy," she said. "He is also very excited that you are connecting with him. He has become a teacher. He is doing the work of welcoming others who have crossed the rainbow bridge, and he shows them which way to go. He tells me he is very glad that you had written the original *Brighton Morning* book about him. He also says he loves

---

[4] Ragan, Lynn, *Signs From Pets in the Afterlife – Identifying Messages From Pets in Heaven* (Atlanta, GA: Afterlife Communications, 2015), 83-84.

all the things you have been doing for him during his life and beyond."

What was an especially significant message from the animal communicator was the depth of our love. "Brighton was definitely an old soul, and so are you. In past lives, you and Brighton may have perhaps even shared a special romantic love," she said.

This was extremely confirming, and I affirmed, "Oh, that makes so much sense to me. I had always felt Brighton was an old soul, and at times I would refer to him as a Yoda."

The animal communicator asked me what I had wanted to know from Brighton. I paused in a feeling of deep love, and said, "I just want to know that he is okay."

Her final message was of profound importance to me. She said, "What you learned through Brighton was the feeling of divine love!"

In amazement and with a feeling of grace, I exclaimed, "That is it! Divine! I have been using that word more and more in trying to describe the inspired guidance I have felt in writing this book about sharing unconditional love with Brighton."

In seeking deeper understanding of appearance of signs in the afterlife, I sought several books that explained the afterlife experience. I have included a list of references at the end of this book. There was one book that provided many examples of afterlife experiences. It is *After Death Signs from Pet Afterlife and Animals in Heaven* by Brent Atwater, an animal medium.

Atwater provided enlightenment on a fascinating dynamic called "over soul agreements." In over-souling, the deceased pet in heaven directs and guides the living animal on what to do and how to behave. It is a contract made between the deceased pet and the living animal, and the deceased pet's energy visits the living animal. A pet being "over-souled" makes you think "he acts like my old pet," by displaying recognizable and very identifiable characteristics. I have observed such phenomena with a sense of deep questioning. Snowdon has displayed behaviors that are different from before and that often resemble Brighton's characteristic nuances. He often begs now like Brighton used to. Also, on walks, Snowdon used to stroll in an amiable, free-spirited way, while now he will stop and plop and refuse to move, in a way that is very similar to Brighton. There have also been little instances where I look at Snowdon and think he actually barks like and resembles Brighton!

Some mysterious phenomena had occurred the day before Brighton's death. I had put my hands on him while anointing him with the song "See Me, Feel Me." When I removed my hands, I discovered that Brighton's fur had mysteriously become very wet with no explanation. Atwater does an enlightening job of explaining the transition process, including potential signs leading up to the time for transition. A "memory moment" is an action or behavior that is out of character for the way your pet normally behaves or acts. It is the pet's way of acknowledging and honoring the love between you as they complete that particular earthly lifetime. A "memory moment" is also your pet's way of letting you know that everything is okay—no matter what happens—and that he *knows* what's going on and that he will be fine after finishing the transition process! Learning of this mystical dynamic has given me tremendous peace. It may also explain the mysterious wetness in his fur that I had felt after removing my hands.

Several books provided additional examples of signs from the afterlife. Atwater provides an extensive overview of almost forty examples.[5] I have personally experienced over half of those items. Including the following:

Books	Coincidences	Ducks	Hearts
Blackbird	Crying	Feathers	Numbers
Cardinal	Dove	Flowers	Rainbow
Clouds	Electronics	Frog	Songs/Music
Coin	Energy Presence	Geese	Wind Chime

SNOW SIGNS

This is the special portrait of Brighton that was done by an

---

[5] Atwater, Brent, *After Death Signs from Pet Afterlife and Animals in Heaven.* (Monee, IL: Just Plain Love Books, 2018).

artist in Wales. Doc talks about Brighton like he is still here. It is somewhat confusing to me when she puts the crystal doggie on the foyer floor in the sunlight. Then she points to colored dots on my paws and on my face and, in a sweet voice, says, "Aw, Brighton's giving you a kiss. Look, Snowdon! Look at the rainbow dots!"

I look at Doc in a confused way, as I admit I am confused. She says Brighton's name, but I just don't see him anymore. Every morning, Doc goes into the living room and opens the shutters by the corner shelves that have pictures of Brighton, and there are always fresh flowers.

Doc will say, "Good morning, Brighton!"

When she greets Brighton, I get a feeling of excitement, which always causes me to bark and bark happily. I don't entirely understand Doc thinking that Brighton is there, but she points to the large picture of him on the wall, and I can feel that Doc believes he is there. Maybe my excitement and barking is me feeling him too? I'm just not sure.

When we go out for our early morning walk, I often stop in the driveway right where a huge beam of sun is shining on the blacktop. For some reason, I decide to stop and ponder. Doc pulls my leash for me to come along, and I finally get going. As I start to sniff along the grass, a bird high up in the tree will start chirping loudly. Doc will excitedly greet Brighton.

"Good morning, Brighton! Oh, Brighton, I can't see you up in the tree. Where are you? I hear you, Brighton."

We stop so Doc can stand strangely in the middle of the street and look up high, twisting her head up and around, trying to see a red cardinal. Strange things sometimes happen during our morning walks. Doc and I will often stroll through a large beam of sunlight on the sidewalk and grass. We will have to stop, and Doc will start talking to the sunbeam! Now me, I am totally a sniffing guy. Light beams just don't do it for me! So, we look like quite a pair with Doc looking up and talking to the sunbeam and me ignoring the whole thing and making deep sniffs on the grass from the markings of other dogs. Doc will often look at a shadow on the grass in the middle of the sunbeam and talk to it like she was talking to Brighton, saying, "Aw, thank you, Brighton, for the hug."

Whatever...

Our living room is so full of scents of Brighton that it seems somewhat natural that he is still here. There are always flowers that smell, and the rugs and dog bed that were in the room still remain. Now, though, an empty space replaces what I used to always feel as my buddy beside me. I would always sense some other movement, or often, Brighton would start barking out of nowhere. Now I am alone resting on the floor, waiting for Doc to give me some attention.

Doc calls me to go upstairs with her almost every day, and we spend time on the bed by the window and get excited if the bright sunlight shines on us! While Doc showers and gets ready, she scatters some kibble in the library and I have to go hunting to find treats. Brighton was not able to go upstairs for a long time, as he had trouble climbing the stairs. So now that I can freely go up and down and in and out of the rooms, I feel I have a special privilege that is fun, but not as much fun without Brighton.

It is just not the same doing things by myself without Brighton around. The play and competition was something I just thought was always part of my life. I know Doc is trying very hard to give me extra attention since I am now alone. Now Doc has to be my playmate, and we spend more time outside on walks. I can't help it, however, that I miss not having another dog as my special pack. Doc is great, but she's not as much fun as a dog buddy. When we meet people on our walks, I hear Doc telling them about Brighton and that I miss my buddy. She is right.

SONG INSPIRATION

"To Where You Are" (by Josh_Groban)

There have been several times when I experienced deaths in my life, and I seemed to have become aware of a particular song as a message of connection. When Pops's mother passed some years ago, the song "Wind Beneath My Wings" kept appearing frequently and seemed like a message.

I also attended a profound funeral for a young mother who had died, leaving behind a husband and three school-age children. That sad experience kept haunting me in my concern for the family. I had been in a gift shop one day and became aware that a song had been repeatedly playing over the sound system in the store. I stopped and listened carefully to each word of the song and wrote down the refrain that I sensed was the profound message.

For the next week, I began to search through songs and finally found the mysterious one I had accidentally heard in the shop! It was by a young rising artist who I had not known. His name was Josh Groban. The song was like a voice connecting a loved one on earth with a spirit in heaven! The title was "To Where You Are." I sent a CD with the song to the husband of the young mother who had passed, with a note explaining the message I saw in the lyrics. At times, I have also sent the Josh Groban CD to others who are grieving the loss of a family member.

The title of the song is "To Where You Are." It begins very slowly, expressing a conundrum of whether the loved one's spirit may still be near. It goes on to honor being surrounded in remembrance. Love is affirmed in the verse that inspires the belief in an invisible power. The emotional refrain is a plea to connect again with our beloved angel in heaven. Now, the song applies to me in connecting with my sweet angel, Brighton.

8

• •

Adios, Yet Not Goodbye

The movie *Racing in the Rain* was released on August 9, 2019, a month after Brighton's thirteenth birthday. This was just four weeks before Brighton received his cancer diagnosis. I had read the book *The Art of Racing in the Rain* many years ago when it had first been published. The story was always so profound for me, as it was written in the voice of the golden retriever, Enzo.

As soon as the movie was released, I knew I had to see it! I was also certain that It would be extremely sad for me. From the beginning of the story, the audience knows Enzo will die at the end. So, I made up my mind to see the movie alone in a theater. I went to the first showing of the film at ten in the morning, and there was only one other person in the theater. I bought a comforting tub of popcorn and sat back to absorb the movie, with tissues ready in case I shed tears throughout the film. As anticipated, the movie did make me cry. Yet, I also deeply absorbed several messages in the various subplots of Enzo's story.

What struck me more than ever in *Racing in the Rain* was the message of reincarnation and how a soul returns, sometimes at a higher level. Enzo explains early in the story that he has become so wise in human ways that he is ready to return as a person. At the end of the movie, he does return as a little boy named Enzo, with a passion for following Enzo's dad, Denny, who has moved to Italy and has realized his dream of becoming a Formula I race car driver for the Ferrari team.

The reincarnation message resonated in me very strongly, as my intuition about Brighton's thirteenth year dominated my mind. I couldn't help but realize the comparable limitations in Enzo and Brighton's lives. I knew the release of the movie and the message from Enzo was a gift to me. It registered in my soul as an assurance that Brighton had a destiny ahead of him to transition into spirit and perhaps return in another life.

From the time I first bonded with Brighton as a pup, I had always felt he had the spirit of an old soul. I would often refer to him as my Yoda, and there is a whole chapter in my book *Brighton Morning* about his Yoda spirit. In fact, when choosing his name as a new pup, I had fastidiously whittled weeks of research down to two final choices, either Brighton or Yoda. I finally chose the name Brighton, as it was more fitting for a pup, and it was the perfect name. I had the intuition that he had the destiny to "Brighton" the lives of everyone he met.

Little did I recognize during the time Brighton was a pup what I somehow understand now. The animal communicator had confirmed in my session that Brighton and I were both old souls and had a romantic love, possibly in a previous lifetime. I have been doing significant reading related to animals and the afterlife, and some of the inspired authors have also mentioned that pets may reincarnate. They may not actually return as the same pet; however, examples show how they can be recognized through similarities that are clues that we are reconnecting with our pets who have returned in an earthly identity.

My significant research relates to other cultures, and I am aware that there are spiritual beliefs in some cultures that involve reincarnation. My personal childhood was integrated in a very Catholic home, based on traditional Catholic tenets. Rencarnation was not part of my belief system. When I was a little girl, I loved to dance. I would often retreat into our basement and play music very loudly and freely twirl around the room. As I approached adolescence, for some odd reason, I especially became passionate about the exquisite heritage that was part of the tapestry of the traditions of Spain.

I became especially fixated in my early teen years with an extended 101 strings version of the beautiful orchestra piece "Malaguena." When I was home alone, I would loudly play it over and over and move around the room to the music. Somehow, the sound of the stringed instruments would reverberate with the strings in my heart.

As a teenage girl, it puzzled me why I was so drawn to that particular Spanish song. I would also read about other aspects of the culture of Spain, beyond what I was studying in my four years of high school Spanish classes. When I was an adult and visited the country of Spain, I felt such a connection to Flamenco dance, El Cid, and the exquisite castles of Spain. I especially identified with Don Quixote, the Man of La Mancha, and felt my own soul was connected to the words of the song "The Impossible Dream." As an adult, I would often humorously think that perhaps I had been a lady of Spain in a previous life.

An amazing coincidence happened during the time I began putting this book into writing. The elusive story of Brighton's final journey had, for months, been carved in my heart and mind. After Brighton passed, I connected on Facebook with an angel friend who amazingly understood me so deeply in terms of my forever connection with Brighton. She had experienced the same depth of grief in the loss of her golden retriever, Max.

This friend became my twinship soul. She has a deep passion for horses and is also challenged with a chronic medical condition that led to her hospitalization during the time I was writing the book. To inspire her recovery, I would find songs from YouTube that I sensed would provide her with healing meditation. I especially searched on YouTube for songs that connected with her passion for horses.

My random YouTube searches generated an exquisite horse performance with a classic Spanish horseman riding a golden horse into a Spanish bullring. When the horse and rider reach the center of the ring, they meet a flamboyant Flamenco dancer. The horseman guides the exquisite stallion to a dance with the Flamenco dancer. They execute an enchanting and totally amazing dance performance to Willie Nelson and Julio Iglesias singing "Spanish Eyes."

At the end of the song, the horseman disappears, and then there is a transition to his returning to the ring, leading a magnificent white stallion. The symbolism struck me as most profound. I was thrilled with the original dance performance, and I shared the song on Facebook and with my twinship friend. Then I viewed the reentry of the exquisite white stallion, mirroring a dream I had always had of someday owning a white Lipizzaner stallion. I always loved the famous white stallions of the Spanish riding school. I began to play "Spanish Eyes" over and over, until I sensed an intuitive message from Brighton that enlightened my soul.

The video of the Flamenco dancer and the Spanish rider on the horse became a mystical image of my relationship with Brighton! I was the lady of Spain as the Flamenco dancer, and Brighton was the golden horse. I realized that our life together was a beautiful dance of artistry and love. We each maintained our unique identity, yet together, we were living as dynamic partners in a beautiful dance of life. Together we "Brighton'd" the lives of everyone we'd meet.

What was truly amazing was the end of the video! The Spanish horseman reenters the arena leading the magnificent stallion that returns in a white form, almost like a Pegasus! When the white stallion reaches the center of the ring near the dancer, he takes a majestic bow by gracefully making a movement down to his knees. This, to me, is a symbol of Brighton returning in spirit and taking another bow! The message of the song "Spanish Eyes" was a story of two old souls. Brighton and I had danced through this life together, and we were now transitioning beyond into the bond of eternal life together!

SONG INSPIRATION

"Spanish Eyes" (by Willie Nelson and Julio Iglesias)

I was able to see a magical connection in the song "Spanish Eyes." First, I have blue eyes. Plus, my loss of Brighton has led to my shedding many tears. Then, with my spiritual lens in focus on the afterlife, I could see the interpretation of "see you soon," rather than "goodbye." The song inspires a promise of returning and reconnecting with a heart full of love. The message of the refrain is a fervent plea for "Yes!" I will wait and keep looking for the return of Brighton!"

Also, in writing this chapter, I had accompanied Pops to a local jewelry store as we needed batteries replaced in several watches. While standing at the display case in discussion with the jeweler, my eyes casually scanned a display of gemstone rings. Suddenly, amid a field of colorful gemstones, an exquisite ring popped out at me! Pops noticed my fixation on it, and he also looked at the ring. It was almost as if it had spoken to me! Pops suggested that I try it on. I hesitated, as I knew my finger was too large and that it would not fit.

I had recently discussed with Pops a plan to have my original diamond engagement ring remounted into a new and appropriately sized ring. The beautiful gemstone ring in question was a blue London topaz stone completely surrounded by tiny diamonds. The ring would be equivalent to a contemporary diamond engagement ring, but the center stone was blue topaz. I slid the ring halfway up my ring finger and became enamored with it. My husband asked the jeweler if the ring could be resized, and the jeweler said he would check and get back to us.

A week later, it happened to be my birthday, and we returned to the jewelry store to pick up the watches we had left for battery replacement. As we stood waiting at the glass display case, the jeweler walked over with a small leather box in his hand. Both my husband and the jeweler were grinning. They conspired, without me knowing, to have the beautiful ring sized to fit my ring finger as a new engagement ring! I was truly shocked and enchanted!

The new ring was a perfect gift. It was more symbolic than any of us could fully know! Topaz is traditionally more of a blue-green color, yet this topaz stone was such a deep, deep blue, with just a slight tinge of deep turquoise. Plus, it was an oval stone mounted in a nontraditional horizontal mount, so it literally could be interpreted as an eye! The large topaz was surrounded by tiny diamonds and could be viewed as sparkling eyelashes surrounding the eye! Since I had been playing the song "Spanish Eyes" so frequently, I soon realized that the new ring was a jeweled metaphor of a blue Spanish eye! I now wear the ring every day and frequently stop to glance at my blue Spanish-eye ring. It is a sparkling reminder of the romantic love I share with Pops.

This chapter has the title "Adios and Not Goodbye!" Perhaps it is no coincidence that the timing has such significance. If we look at a pregnancy as nine months, it took nine months for me to come to this point in writing of Brighton's forever journey. He transitioned across the rainbow bridge on December 9! Nine months from the time of his passing would bring us full circle to a year since he first was diagnosed with spleen cancer.

It was three months after Brighton's passing that the world suddenly became engulfed in the disruption of the COVID-19 pandemic. I had been closely following the spread of the virus in Europe, as Pops had purchased airline tickets to travel there in May. In planning the impending trip to Europe, we had considered a return visit to Brighton and Snowdon's breeder in the Netherlands. I always liked to follow the progress of the new Morning Valley English Crème golden litters, as they all contain some DNA from Brighton's pedigree.

The next litter was due to be born in April, and, in fact, the pups were born on Easter Sunday. But the pups had all been reserved, plus the COVID pandemic had created a looming uncertainty about the prospect of shipping pups to the United States. At that time, I expressed interest in the next available litter. It turned out that a female and male bearing a strong pedigree background to Brighton had been mated the day after Easter.

The breeder warmly responded that the standard policy was not to accept a deposit until the litter was born, as the number of pups available was unknown. I expressed my interest and was advised to wait until early June to place a deposit once the pups arrived. In the meantime, April and May passed with the whole world shut down from COVID-19. Plus, there was uncertainty as to the possibility of international travel. Overseas shipment of a pup was also questionable within the restraints of the pandemic.

I am totally dedicated to following our Netherlands' breeder on Facebook. So, I waited for her announcement that the new litter expected in early June was born. Within a day of that announcement, I sent her a private Facebook message, asking about the availability of a pup and for the instructions to formally place a deposit. To my immediate disappointment, all the pups had already been formally reserved prior to my message. There was such a meaning for me in the existence of Brighton's pedigree in these pups. Therefore, our breeder promised to check and see if anyone who had reserved a pup would be willing to wait until the next litter that was due to be born in August and free up a male pup for me.

It was a blessing to receive a text two days later that the breeder was able to arrange it, which would free up a male pup! Hurray! The pups had been born on June 10, six months since the passing of Brighton! The pup would be shipped from the Netherlands at ten weeks of age, which would be almost nine months since Brighton's transition and almost a year since his original tumor diagnosis!

The deep significance of the movie *Racing in the Rain* continued in my mind. I had integrated the message expressed throughout the film about the imagination of returning in reincarnation. Recently, I had been reading several books about the pet afterlife. I learned that even if a pet does return in some form, it is not done quickly and not necessarily to the original owner. Nevertheless, my excitement was palpable at the anticipation of receiving a pup bearing Brighton's direct DNA heritage in the pup's pedigree! The words of the song "Spanish Eyes" also included the message of waiting for a return of the beloved.

Brighton's story has been guided on its angel journey by the message provided in the movie *Racing in the Rain* that I had seen just a year before. Then there was the synchronicity with the song

"Spanish Eyes." Things were coming full circle. There was no doubt that the new pup would be named Enzo.

Enzo's pedigree is integrated within the pedigrees of Brighton and Snowdon.

- Enzo's father, Obsidian, is a son of Passionate
- Passionate is Snowdon's sister
- Enzo's father is Snowdon's nephew
- Enzo is Snowdon's grandnephew
- Snowdon's father is Enzo's grandfather
- Enzo's great-great-grandfather, Dream Max, was Brighton's father.
- Enzo's great-great-great-grandmother, Lourdes, was Brighton's mother.

It will be for the mystic to interpret whether Enzo is actually a reincarnation of Brighton. Nevertheless, Brighton's DNA heritage would be returning to our home soon!

SNOW WAITING

Doc and Pops keep talking about something called COVID. All I know is that we go on longer walks, but it is not the same walking without my doggie buddy, Brighton. On our walks along the path and the sidewalk by the street, we often see people and other dogs. Yet, Doc pulls me aside so I can't get any nearer than probably a car's distance away. I want so badly to go back to the old days when we would walk with Brighton and meet other dogs to sniff. We would often meet other people, and, once I knew it was okay, I would jump up and try to gently hug them. I loved being very friendly.

Now it feels like everyone has the canine flu. Brighton and I had that one time, and we could not get near any other dogs. It was a bummer. Now, even Doc stays away from other people, and they are wearing masks! When we do stop to talk to people, I must stay farther away, and people seem to avoid getting close. You'd think I was contagious or something! I hear Doc telling people about how we miss Brighton, which is very true. She looks at me sadly and tells them that I am lonesome. Yes, I am!

We've had a hot boring summer, home all the time, and staying away from everyone. Doc tries hard to play with me, and we go on lonesome long walks four times a day. I have never done so much sniffing and marking in my whole life! To make me feel less lonesome, Doc sometimes shows me videos of other dogs on her phone. The problem is that I get so excited seeing other dogs that I bark loudly and it upsets Pops. Doc even got a weird little machine. When I start to bark, she holds it up with a little red light looking my way. Suddenly, each bark triggers a strong sound. Doc can't hear it, but I do, and it makes me stop barking and move away. This combination of missing Brighton and COVID is a real bummer! Life is doggone different!

For Doc's birthday, she received two big pots of flowers, and each had a floating balloon trying to drift up to the sky. Pops also got Doc a pretty ring, and I would hear them mention it a lot. Then one day, a huge box arrived. That night, Doc opened the box, and I saw it was a folded fence. When Doc and Pops put it together, it turned out to be a dog crate that was not quite as big as mine. They parked the new crate next to the end of mine. It did not mess up my crate area, but I admit I was curious and would sneak and peek inside at a fluffy, new blue dog bed.

Doc keeps talking more and using the word *Enzo*. So what is that? Sometimes Doc says *Enzo* while showing me a puppy picture on her phone. I start to bark excitedly. Somehow, the way she says Enzo is like saying, "Do you want to go out?" or "Want to go to Paws?" I somehow am getting the idea that Enzo has something to do with it!

Now, it was a matter of waiting all summer for Enzo's arrival. He was born on June 10 but would not be ready to ship to the United States until at least eight to ten weeks of age, which would be around the third week in August. In the meantime, we received photos of little Enzo as he happily pranced around the beautiful Morning Valley paradise with his mama, Lemon, and seven other littermates. One video posted on Facebook showed the whole litter gathered around their breeder mom as she was sharing a bag of treats. Suddenly, she sees one pup is missing, and turns around to call a pup who was away at the far fence, exploring on his own. When she called, he charged ahead, bounding along with a puppy gait to catch up. That was Enzo! Another video showed him all wet in the wading pool. His breeder mom said he was perfect for us, as he was extremely sweet and gentle.

9

• •

Circuit of Bright

It was the circuit of another year that began in September. It was a band of a journey paved in the gold of an English crème golden retriever named Brighton. The circuit was a spiral that was spun in a profound integration of three-month segments. The prelude was the three months of summer that included a delightful staycation at Brighton's beloved paws paradise, the celebration of Brighton's thirteenth birthday, and one last paws staycation with waning months unexpectedly just over the horizon.

The tear-jerking movie *Racing in the Rain* was also released late that summer. The story of the film's golden retriever, Enzo, emerged as a metaphoric vision of a circle of life in a racing circuit. The looming finish line was like a glooming prediction seemingly foreshadowed in the reincarnation message of a movie.

THREE MONTH CIRCUITS

(3 Months—2019) Prelude
June 6   Seventy-Fifth Anniversary D-Day France
July 4   Brighton's thirteenth birthday
August   Last staycation boarding at paws paradise

(3 Months—2019)
September 5   Diagnosis of spleen tumor
October 15   Brighton crisis illness (recovered)
November   Last Thanksgiving
December 9   Rainbow bridge, age 13.5 years

(3 Months—2020)
January   Visit Houston—Snowdon at paws paradise
February   Beginning of COVID-19 pandemic
March   Contact with Morning Valley re: a new pup

(3 Months—2020)
April   Lemon/Jason mated—Easter Monday
May   COVID-19 isolation—United States and Europe
June 10   Lemon Litter—Enzo born

(3 Months—2020)
July 4   Brighton's fourteenth birthday in heaven
August   Plans for Enzo's arrival
September 1   Enzo's arrival from Morning Valley
September 21   Sudden loss of Pops

Morning Valley

The Morning Valley Kennel in the Netherlands was the birthplace of Brighton and Snowdon. It held a special place in our hearts. In summer 2012, Pops and I visited the Netherlands and Morning Valley. It was located about three hours northeast of Amsterdam. We spent an entire afternoon with our beloved breeder, enjoying the outdoors of the large, beautiful property of Morning Valley. It was such a picturesque Dutch country house and a golden retriever heaven. During our visit, I took many photos of all the beautiful Morning Valley dogs that were relatives of Brighton. Sheer Magic (Hazel) was especially fond of Pops, and to this day, we have in our home a treasured framed picture of them together. Hazel was to eventually be Enzo's great-grandmother. We also had the special excitement of meeting Brighton's father, Nielson (Dream Max an Apple a Day), an international champion with a legacy of litters.

We left Morning Valley with a very special love for Brighton's heritage that had grown into a family passion. After our visit, I kept in touch and made arrangements to reserve a puppy from the litter to be born at Christmas. That was Snowdon, who was born on December 23, 2012. Snowdon was shipped later in February at eight weeks old, and that truly sealed our deep dedication to the Morning Valley pedigree.

Throughout Brighton's last year, I followed Morning Valley on Facebook. I learned from a February posting that there was a litter due around Easter and sent an email inquiry about the availability of a pup. Unfortunately, the litter to be born on Easter had already been completely reserved. The next litter would be from the mating of Lemon and Jason on the day after Easter, and the pups would be due in early June. That quickly emerged as an evolving plan. It seemed rather symbolic that the mating for the litter of our next pup took place on Easter Monday. How ironic to have a sign of resurrection, rebirth, and rising from the dead. The legacy and spirit of Brighton continued in his DNA destiny.

The pedigree of the mother, Lemon (Arrival of the Morning Valley), and the father, Jason (Obsidian of the Morning Valley) was perfect. I had developed such a deep love for the Morning Valley lineage that it seemed sheer destiny that Brighton's heritage was carved deep in the pedigree of this litter. To convey my excitement with the connection to Brighton, I had to make a complicated chart. It shows so many connections that I found it necessary to split the chart into two sections. The first chart shows the pedigree of Enzo on his mother's side. How exciting that Lemon's great-grandfather was Brighton's father. Lemon's great-great-grandmother was Brighton's mother, Lourdes! On the father's side, Jason is the son of Snowdon's sister, so Enzo's father is Snowdon's nephew, and Snowdon is Enzo's great-uncle! In addition, Brighton's mother is also Enzo's great-great-great-grandmother on the father's side. This litter seemed genetically to be a spiraling destiny.

Enzo (Slice of Lemon Morning Valley)
Born June 10, 2020
MV of the Morning Valley

Parents	**LEMON** (Arrival – MV)	Enzo's mother
	JASON (Obsidian – MV)	Enzo's Father –
		Snowdon's Nephew
Grand-Parents	**Midnight Sun - MV**	Enzo's grandmother
	Noah of Hallacious Acres	Enzo's grandfather
	Passion (Passionate – MV)	Enzo's grandmother
		Snowdon's sister
		(Snowdon - grand uncle)
Great Grand-Parents	**Majik Truth or Dare** (**Snowdon's** father)	Enzo's great grandfather
	Sheer Magic - MV	Enzo's great-grandmother
	Lady Apple – MV (**Snowdon's** mother)	Enzo's great-grandmother
Great-Great Grand-Parents	**Nielson (Dream Max An Apple A Day)** (**Brighton's** father)	Enzo's great-great grandfather
	Bliss of Morning Valley (**Snowdon** grandmother)	Enzo's great-great-grandmother
Great-Great-Great Grand-Parents	**Snowdon** - MV	Enzo's great-great-great-grandfather
	Lourdes - MV (**Brighton's** mother)	Enzo's great-great-great-grandmother (Snowdon's grandmother)

- Enzo's great-uncle is Snowdon
- Enzo's great-great-great-grandmother is Brighton's mother and Snowdon's grandmother
- Enzo's great-grandfather is Snowdon's father
- Enzo's great-great-grandfather is Brighton's father

Pandemic and Quarantine

Snowdon had never quite acted the same after Brighton's passing. It was obvious that we all felt a void in the house. Snowdon had lost his buddy, when they would often be together, side by side, taking turns getting one kibble treat at a time. Now, there was no competition for Snowdon, but it was also obvious that there was no company. It seemed being given sole attention was not as important to Snowdon as having a fur buddy companion of his own kind. There was no doggone sense of playful fun! What made the loneliness worse for all of us was the COVID-19 pandemic, where we had to keep social distancing from people and other animals.

Enzo—Born June 10

The day that Lemon and Jason's new litter was born was just a year after we had spent such a profound week at Omaha Beach area in Normandy to participate in a week's events commemorating the seventy-fifth anniversary of D-Day. The Morning Valley website displayed a perfect photo of Mama Lemon and her litter of five girls and three boys. How I hoped one of the boys would be ours.

Circuit of Bright— Starting Line

Enzo was originally scheduled to be shipped to us from Amsterdam during the third week in August, when he was ten weeks old. At that time, we were experiencing some medical circumstances related to a hospital test for Pops. Thankfully, Morning Valley was able to reschedule Enzo's shipment for September 1. Also, the last two weeks in August were extremely hot in Amsterdam, as well as in Chicago. International airline regulations prohibit animals from being shipped if the outdoor heat at either airport is above eighty degrees. With the medical appointment scheduled for Pops in Chicago, it seemed a grace that the shipment of our pup would not be until September l, when Enzo was eleven weeks old.

Ten days prior to his scheduled arrival, I started posting clues on Facebook, giving hints of the surprise that was to come in chapter 10 of this book. For several days, I provided different versions of the song "Circle of Life." I called special attention to the lyrics of the song, which included a significant message in the lyrics with the words *faith* and *hope*. I recall how hope and faith had been key themes during Brighton's three-month journey toward the rainbow bridge.

The arrival date for Enzo approached, and an anxious anticipation permeated our home. We purchased a new crate and pad that was designed to be used in the back of our SUV. We also ordered a second large crate as Enzo's new safe place at home. There was never a consideration of taking away Snowdon's crate. The new crate would be positioned adjacent to Snowdon's. Everything would be planned to make the addition of the new pup as smooth as possible for Snowdon. The new crate was put into place over a week prior to Enzo's arrival, and I would sometimes point to the crate and tell Snowdon it was for Enzo.

That summer in 2020, we were living under the daunting COVID-19 regulations for protection against exposure to the virus. I had put together my own protection kit of airline arrival items, including rubber gloves, disinfectant wipes, paper towels, and plastic bags. I had received advice from friends to be cautious in wiping off the airline crate and taking care to use disinfectant wipes on any items that might have been touched. It was important to kill any germs that might have been transported in the flight from Amsterdam.

It was almost as if my car knew the way to KLM Cargo at O'Hare International Airport. Again, the larger pattern of a circuit was emerging throughout the entire process. Fourteen years earlier, on September 15, I first navigated my way to the back entrance of this huge international airport to find the air cargo receiving area for KLM airlines. That was the day I had picked up Brighton, and I distinctly recall him in the air freight terminal, sitting quietly inside the airline crate, looking sheepishly at me with a lost expression.

My second trip to the same KLM Cargo location was six and a half years later when I picked up Snowdon. That experience was a clue that Snowdon was a much more gregarious personality than sweet Brighton. While waiting in the front office of KLM Cargo for our final paperwork to be cleared, I had gone into an adjacent restroom. Suddenly, I heard this loud and consistent barking that made me stop and think! I asked myself, "Could that be my pup barking in such a way that it could be heard all the way into the restroom?"

Yes, barking was my first introduction to Snowdon! From the moment I opened Snowdon's airline crate and placed it in the back seat of our SUV, he never stopped barking! I remember driving home in slow rush-hour traffic and listening to his barking the entire way. I phoned my breeder friend while driving, and she became a witness to the hysterical puppy humor of my driving with nonstop barking for almost an hour in rush-hour traffic.

The circuit of the KLM Cargo trip was again repeated the summer of Brighton's final year, when I had joined a breeder from Arkansas to welcome her new Morning Valley pup. I remember feeling a sense of confusion inside. I had such a love for Morning Valley that the thought had crossed my mind to have bought the puppy myself. Yet, there was no way I could add a puppy to our home. Due to my intense loyalty to Brighton, I would not take away any time that I needed to devote to my gradually aging boy. Although I had no indication at that time that Brighton had a pending end-of-life medical condition, I knew from his age of thirteen that the hourglass of his life was approaching empty. I was able to hold the pup named Fahrenheit on that arrival date, and somehow, I sensed a circuit of new life in my arms, even as the circuit of a waning life was also permeating my heart.

Now, I was on my fourth journey to KLM Cargo! As I had dreaded the summer before, Brighton had crossed the rainbow bridge. Nine months later, I was picking up Enzo, the carrier of Brighton's DNA and the completion of a circuit in my life. The pick-up on September 1 was literally a cloudy experience. It was raining hard that day. The flight from Amsterdam had arrived on time. However, due to the extreme heat of the previous two weeks, there were a large number of postponed dog arrivals scheduled on that flight. Plus, this time it was during the COVID-19 pandemic. Regulations related to travel or waiting in line required use of facemasks, wiping of hands, and social distancing with at least six feet between anyone in line.

I arrived early at the KLM Cargo area, planning plenty of time. I entered the waiting area to check on what needed to be done to pick up my new pup, Enzo. Due to social distancing, I was told to wait in my car and come back in an hour. When I returned an hour later, there were several other people ahead of me. With only two allowed inside the waiting room at a time, the rest were lined up six feet apart in the lobby hallway.

The small foyer area became a snaking line with the required six-foot spacing that began to stretch out the door. Since there had been two weeks of hot weather, many other overseas dog transports had also been postponed. A dozen animal shipments were now being held in the US Customs area after the plane had landed. Processing of dogs shipped from overseas generally takes about an hour with passport clearance and registration and US Customs paperwork. The dogs also need to be examined by a USDA veterinarian, and vaccination paperwork verified, along with import quarantine instructions.

With the number of owners and breeders waiting, some for multiple dogs, it was over two hours from the time the plane landed until owners' names were being called. Coping with the long wait, finally I was called up to the counter and was provided with paperwork to sign, plus payment of an additional airport handling fee. Then I was directed to a doorway leading to the back receiving area. It was a huge, open area, containing large sections of boxes and shipping crates. Halfway down the area I could see several animal crates, and a staff member directed me to go to the parking lot and bring my vehicle around to the loading dock. I still had not seen my pup and had barely seen his crate in the distant section of the holding area.

It was another ten minutes by the time I rushed to retrieve my vehicle. Finally, I was able to arrive at the loading dock to drive my SUV backward up a ramp the length of a semi-trailer. Two workmen were carrying an obviously heavy animal crate around to the rear of my SUV and, as quickly as they could, they shoved it in the back and directed me to exit as soon as possible, as other pick-ups were coming. I also remembered to ask them to check that the passport was affixed to the crate, and it was tucked into an envelope tightly attached to the crate with duct tape. I slowly drove my SUV down the extended ramp. Making a U-turn to find an open spot in the parking lot, I was finally able to allow my pup his overdue freedom. What in my mind should have been a momentous meeting so far had been basically a shipping package pick-up! So much for sentimentality!

I finally was able to back into a parking lot space up against a grassy meridian area. I grabbed my sanitary supplies of vinyl gloves, paper towels, disinfectant wipes and plastic bags. Now, the anticipation of the moment of meeting Enzo had turned into a sanitary scenario. I opened the hatch and turned the gate side of the airline crate outward. Of all things, the gate had been fastened to the crate with heavy plastic binding straps that could only be released by cutting with a scissors or knife. In my thoughtful planning of the welcome supplies, I had not included scissors! I stood there looking into the crate. There, cringing in the far corner of the crate, was Enzo, looking quite stunned and not wanting to move. In frustration, I phoned Pops, always there as my rescue. I had to use his shipping expertise for an idea of how to cut the fastening. His immediate and pragmatic response was that I would need to go back to the receiving dock and ask one of the dock workmen to cut the bands for me! Oh no!

It was another fifteen minutes before I would finally be able to even fully see my precious Enzo! I drove back to the dock, and an understanding workman did cut the bands for me. Then I closed the hatch and drove back to the parking spot by the grassy meridian. Finally, I was able to open the hatch and open the gate of the crate! There, cringing in the far corner was poor, exhausted Enzo. He was sitting in a pile of shredded newspaper, showing total fear of moving. I started softly talking to him and slowly guiding my arm back to touch him and coax him out of the crate. It appeared that he was afraid to even get up and move his back legs, and I realized that I would need to pull him out with a slow, gentle tug. Along with my grasp came the urine-soiled shredded newspaper. It was quite wet but not soggy. Once he was out of the crate, I could pull the paper clear and see that fortunately, his rear end was not badly soiled.

Finally, I was able to pull Enzo into my arms! My goodness, he was big and heavy, just as his breeder had told me. I wrapped my arms around him and hugged him tightly for several minutes, just rocking him back and forth. He looked squarely into my eyes, and I looked into what I felt was the family legacy of my sweet Brighton. Somehow, I feel that first look we exchanged will stay with both of us forever. It also solidified a bond that I realized would be a constant sealed attachment between us for endless time to come!

Prior to the arrival day, I had purchased a new wire crate designed in a thin version to fit into the back of an SUV. Luckily, I had already placed that wire crate in the SUV, and I had lined the bottom with an older dog bed that had belonged to Brighton. With the airline crate still containing soiled shredded newspaper, I realized that, using COVID-19 precautions, I would need to wipe it out to disinfect it from any germs that might have been carried over from the Netherlands. It was a grace that I was able to put Enzo into the new crate instead of back into the soiled one.

Enzo and I had bonded in a long hug, and I quickly realized with trepidation that he did not wear any collar or leash! By chance, I had brought a flimsy, temporary leash that had been used at a recent vet appointment. It did not have a collar and was more of a heavy pink ribbon with a loop on one end. It certainly was not the safest collar and leash! In any event, I tenderly stooped down and placed Enzo on the ground to give him a chance to stand and eventually move his hind legs so he could walk and go potty. It was obvious that he had been in that crate for a very long, cramped time. From the time he was locked in the crate at the animal forwarder office in the Netherlands airport, I later calculated it had to be a total of fifteen hours. He was unsure about balancing on his back legs but finally stood and started to give an expected puppy pull toward the grass! We strolled along the parking lot median strip for a short distance, and Enzo was able to walk and leak. He was finally starting to come alive!

Returning to the SUV, I opened the hatch and was thankful I had the new wire crate in the back. I was able to place Enzo safely into a large, contained space that had one of Brighton's cozy dog beds lining the floor. I then took time to use the disinfectant kit I had brought to scoop out the wet paper from the airline crate and wipe everything with disinfectant wipes.

By the time my disinfecting was done, Enzo had started to stand and move within the new crate. At the same time, he started to vigorously come alive and bark with nonstop enthusiasm! When I had picked up Snowdon seven years earlier, he had barked the entire way home. I began to wonder if this would be a repeat performance. The difference was that Enzo was in a large crate where he could sit up and see in all directions. I started to drive, and it was raining heavily. Enzo began to quiet down and curiously began to watch passing cars and scenery. I also remembered that Enzo's breeder mom had been waiting and wondering if he had arrived. So, I pulled over in a gas station to send a quick text saying that Enzo was safe with me. I also sent a text to Pops, who was worrying, reassuring him we were on our way home.

The journey from the airport was in rush-hour traffic, and at times I drove slowly, looking behind me to see Enzo starting to enjoy the ride. By the time we arrived home, it had been over five hours since I had left. Pops and Snowdon had been resigned to waiting and watching for us for such a long time. Pops obviously looked anxious at the long drive I had experienced in the rainstorm during heavy traffic. We had all been extremely curious to see what Snowdon would do. As I parked in our driveway, I anxiously opened the hatch and ceremoniously lifted Enzo out of the crate. Now, he was awake and had become more alert during the long drive. I held the leash and let him quickly take a potty break on our front lawn before approaching the front door.

Pops excitedly opened the front door. Snowdon was crowded right up with his nose at the opening and looked at Enzo with the usual excitement he shows when any visitor arrives and enters our home. Pops was able to warmly greet Enzo, while holding Snowdon. Snowdon's initial reaction of excitement diminished rather quickly. Enzo, by now, was in high gear excitement! He was feeling the joy of being able to move around after fifteen hours in an airline crate, plus an hour's ride home. Now he was being greeted by a white dog that looked just like his mama, Lemon, and the other big dogs at the Morning Valley! He immediately started trying to kiss Snowdon and give him joyful bites on the head and neck! Oh boy, what a shocking experience for poor Snowdon!

The way Enzo joyfully attacked Snowdon was so similar to the way Snowdon had attacked Brighton when Snowdon first came into our home as an eight-week-old pup. I remember that I soon felt sorry for my sweet Brighton when Snowdon continued to bite at him so vigorously. I learned quickly that this was just a pup's way of behaving, but I didn't like seeing my Brighton feeling stressed through a pup attack. Now history was repeating itself, and Snowdon looked as though he was getting his payback! I couldn't help but wonder if Enzo was actually a reincarnated Brighton. It would have been fun for Brighton's spirit to dish out to Snowdon the same puppy menace that Snowdon had delivered to Brighton!

When Snowdon arrived as a puppy, Brighton had already become a very mature and distinguished six-year-old golden retriever, who had gone through mast cell tumor surgery six months before and had been neutered. Plus, Brighton had a certification with the Delta Dog Therapy Society and had made several therapy dog visits to a nursing home and a Ronald McDonald House. Brighton had been the perfect gentleman, and Snowdon quickly became known as the perky punk. Brighton was a reserved role model and older brother to puppy Snowdon. It was an unexpectedly long time before Brighton loosened up a bit to enjoy playing with Snowdon. Now, Snowdon was being similarly reserved upon the surprise arrival of his new puppy brother, Enzo!

The Home Stretch

The first week with Enzo in our home was somewhat uncertain. We had to keep him on a leash, in his wire crate, or confined within an indoor metal fenced yard. We literally could not let Enzo free, as he would immediately attack Snowdon! It reminded us of Cato in the *Pink Panther* movies, when Cato would suddenly jump out and attack Inspector Clouseau! Enzo's attack involved vigorously licking and biting at Snowdon's face, head, and thick fur neck! Frankly, Enzo was brutal with love and enthusiasm. Snowdon would either freeze or slowly back away in disdain. I would intervene to hold Enzo's collar and not let him harm my sweet Snowdon. Sound familiar?

I thought a lot that whole first week about Snowdon's unfriendly reaction toward Enzo. It was not what I had expected. Whenever we had been on walks for the last nine months since

Brighton's passing, Snowdon would often stop, plant himself, and whine when we saw another dog. He acted like he wanted so badly to get close and to play with a dog friend. Now, he was shutting down from any interaction with overfriendly Enzo! I knew Snowdon had appeared to be in grief since Brighton's passing. He had been sleeping more, was always hungry and barking to beg for food, and had shown no zest in his movements or interactions with us. It seemed we had also lost the perky Snowman.

It took a while in writing this book to reflect on Snowdon's grief experience and reaction to Enzo. First, Snowdon had never been without another dog before. There was a buddy energy that another dog was always a part of his existence with Brighton in our home. Now, there was only a void in our whole house. Snowdon could also tell that we missed Brighton, and we would mention his name and display pictures and items to honor and keep Brighton's spirit alive. Snowdon must have sensed this as well.

The beams of light and the daily greetings from a cardinal continued as signs that Brighton was still with us. Perhaps it was very confusing the way I would open the shutters every morning near Brighton's urn and say good morning to Brighton as though he were there. As Brighton had aged and then transitioned into a hospice existence, he had slept a lot more. Now Snowdon was sleeping too much. Brighton would always bark, especially after he could no longer hear, and he was always begging for pieces of kibble as a reward for doing anything. Now, Snowdon was barking like never before, and he kept begging more and more for pieces of his kibble. The barking was hard on Pops.

I realized during the writing of this chapter that Snowdon had, in many respects, taken on Brighton's senior dog behaviors! This reaction had been mentioned in one afterlife book I had read as a possible sign of a spirit connection! I have since recognized that Snowdon's malaise contributed to my grieving the loss of Brighton, and perhaps my grief was a further catalyst for Snowdon's loss of zest. I was witnessing the loss of our perky punk, Snowdon, every day! A doggone double loss!

There were several people who advised me that it would be unwise for us to get a new pup. I listened carefully to their rationale, which all made perfect pragmatic sense. Yet, it was amazing how assured I was of the need for a Morning Valley pup that carried Brighton's pedigree heritage. At times, intuition overrules reason, and we feel a burning desire that defies logic, and this was the case for us. I found myself graciously thanking my caring friends for their advice. Yet, I continued to feel a calling to move ahead with what seemed like an unpopular, maverick decision. It was a calling to maintain the spirit of Brighton in my life. Plus, once Enzo arrived, I realized the decision was also my motherly need to rescue Snowdon's lost livelihood.

Pops had also quietly felt the grief in our home in the loss of Brighton. Yet, he had said he did not want to get another puppy and again have two dogs. When Enzo was born in June, I had to be extremely persuasive to convince Pops to get him. Frankly, one reason was that I could not imagine ever getting to the point of losing Snowdon in old age and then having us left with no dog in our home. Pops had been dealing with medical issues that had slowed him down, plus we were both trapped at home with COVID quarantine observance due to our age. Since we were home all the time, it seemed that the initial stage of training a new pup would provide some positive energy in our trapped existence. Later in the fall, the pup would be older and trained. We had hoped that COVID would have subsided so Pops and I could resume our life, plus travel, using doggie daycare and boarding as needed.

When Enzo first came through our door, there was a definite smile in Snowdon's golden countenance and wagging tail. It was like the excitement he shows whenever any visitor enters the house. Yet, as soon as Enzo began to attack Snowdon with sharp teeth, licks, and kisses, I knew that our grieving Snowdon had been quickly overwhelmed. He stepped back, and I rescued him by holding the squirming and ecstatic Enzo in tight control. This type of scenario lasted for the first week. The best word for Snowdon's reaction was apprehensive and aloof, almost as if he were thinking, "Are you kidding? Who is this punk?"

We would try short moments to put Snowdon and Enzo together, but Enzo's intensity was overwhelming. Snowdon needed to become comfortable with the addition of this gregarious pup into his too-peaceful life. Enzo needed to calm down and be trained to approach Snowdon peacefully.

It took about five days to see any progress between Snowdon and Enzo. Gradually, with collared guidance, Enzo would approach Snowdon's head without diving, kissing, and vigorously chomping at him. We learned that Enzo was definitely a kisser! Snowdon gradually accepted Enzo's nearness. We had received a box of dog toys and treats as a welcoming gift, and that really helped. There were several smaller toys, and both boys became interested in which ones to choose. A couple of the toys were worth fighting over, and that became the icebreaker. Finally, we began to see Snowdon interested in toys again. It had been a long time since he and Brighton had fought over toys, and Snowdon had never liked playing with a toy alone. Due to Snowdon's food allergy restriction, he had been taken off chewing of Nylabone toys, and he would only like soft toys. Yet, he and Brighton would both immediately pull apart the plush toys or try to chew them to pieces (a golden retriever trait).

It was a sense of competitiveness in play that really was the key to bonding! When Snowdon had become so lonesome, I felt he missed the competition. Before Brighton passed, whenever I had given anything to Snowdon, Brighton would immediately perk up and get up to stand right beside Snowdon to get his share. They would take turns with everything. I would give their prescriptive kibble as treats, and it would always be one for Brighton and then one for Snowdon. Even when drinking out of the same water bowl, they would take turns. They watched each other constantly, and if one got attention, the other was right there. So, the loss of that constant "other" in Snowdon's life was profound. It was like trying to play catch or tennis or tug-of-war ... alone.

When Snowdon became intrigued with Enzo's new toys, he quickly began to recover his playful self. Suddenly, closeness and mouth-to-mouth tugging for a toy was fun! It was so amazing to watch big Snowdon beginning to play and wrestle with puppy Enzo. Snowdon seemed to have a sense of restraint in not hurting Enzo, and, in fact, I became more worried watching the voraciousness of Enzo's biting in play. It was up to Snowdon to turn his rear end toward Enzo to deflect the attack. At times, Snowdon would need to use his big mouth to put Enzo in his place. Enzo was a stinker who would pull Snowdon's bushy tail.

Watching Snowdon's gradual reemergence was like watching a tulip bloom as it gradually opens. I had expected a more sudden excitement. Yet, when we had picked up Snowdon and brought him home to meet Brighton, the interface was quite similar. We couldn't help but wonder if Enzo was the reincarnation of Brighton! If so, was Brighton getting back at Snowdon and showing Snowdon how much of a pain in the neck it had been with Snowdon as a pup constantly biting at Brighton? Brighton had been an only dog for six years and had experienced surgery six months before Snowdon had arrived. Snowdon had always been more gregarious in a 24/7 dynamic, until the last year when Brighton was in hospice and after he had crossed the rainbow bridge in December. Snowdon had been forced into a mellowing, aged family dynamic for a year. Now, suddenly there appeared a little guy with the old punk spunk that was more like Snowdon's soul!

During the second week, we watched the tulip open and blossom in Snowdon. He would often watch a few of the toys that became his favorite and would sometimes chew Brighton's moo-cow and chicken. It was funny that there were only a few toys out of the dozen they had that engaged both of them in tug-of-war play. The toys that attracted them both became true bonds of brotherhood. Enzo would take the toy and chew it while watching Snowdon. Snowdon would, at first, act reticent, and I would encourage him to "go get it" and steal the toy back from Enzo. Once Snowdon got the toy, he would savor sprawling out and chomping away at it. Enzo would then start wandering all over and returning to Snowdon, intent on retrieving the treasured toy. This became a steady game by the end of week two. It was such a joy for me to see our punky Snowdon return to us! The dynamic between Enzo and Snowdon also became an affirming sign that Brighton's spirit had returned to our home!

Enzo's barking became our major problem from the time he arrived. He had obviously become attached to me from the moment our eyes had met, when I had first hugged him as I gently guided him out of the airline crate at KLM. I did not realize how deep that bond would be until we were home. I had a crate all set up for him, plus a steel fenced portable yard. As long as he saw me, he was a quiet, lovable puppy. The first couple of days, he snoozed beside me for hours on the couch, and we and Enzo fell in love. As days went on, there were obvious times when I needed to safely put Enzo in his crate or pen area in order to take Snowdon for his walks, take a shower, use the bathroom, cook meals, do laundry, or do a short errand with the car. As soon as I would try to leave Enzo in the supervision of Pops, Enzo would start to bark. This would happen even if I just went to use the bathroom or take a shower. It became such a frustrating situation for Pops!

There was an old puppy trick we had used with Brighton and Snowdon to stop barking. It was a large number of coins we had put in a metal chicken teakettle. When we would shake the chicken, the clanging would startle the dogs and stop the barking. It worked with the standard psychology principle of responding to the bark with an unpleasant, scary sound that the puppy would want to avoid. This worked, but by the third week, the clanging chicken was still necessary, plus we supplemented with a clanging cow bell. We even resorted to a large metal kitchen utensil spoon clanging against the wire crate in quick response to a bark. Enzo knew to stop with the signal, but the behavior was still a steady, uncorrected habit in the third week.

Pops and I were both feeling trapped from COVID restrictions, and as weeks went on, we never felt safe to leave Enzo alone in his crate in the house. It was rather ironic that barking became such an issue, as barking and being afraid to leave had been a problem with Brighton during the last year of his life when he had lost his hearing. I couldn't help but wonder if this was another signal that Brighton's spirit was now in Enzo.

A primary and immediate challenge with any pup is potty training. This training of any pup is expected to be a big job and was one reason others had discouraged me from getting another pup. I went into pup training with as much diligence as possible. With my naïve optimism, I felt that by the end of the first month, Enzo would have acquired a strong connection with eliminating outside. I knew it was part of a pup to have them suddenly squat and wet right in the middle of the floor or on a rug. As it turned out, Enzo had been trained as a pup to wet on newspaper. One of our dog mats was vinyl, and he already went to that mat if he needed to go. I know the potty training is really training for the owner. The first week, Enzo would wake at five in the morning, and I would have to immediately grasp Enzo and whisk him out the door before he could squat and wet. Sometimes I would miss, and sometimes he would miss, and at times he would even come back to the house and then wet the floor inside.

Walking with a lead for the first time was a surprise. Enzo seemed uncomfortable with a collar and leash. It seemed as though he had not had the experience of wearing a collar and walking with a leash. He would weave back and forth in front of me and was totally fascinated with anything that was in the grass. Since it was September when he arrived, there were small leaves beginning to fall on the grass and walkways, and he wanted to eat every leaf he could. In fact, being a typical puppy, he wanted to eat anything he could! I would catch him chewing and open his mouth to scoop out a small portion of a twig or a small bead of blacktop from the street surface.

Enzo reminded me of Brighton, who had always been the best scavenger ever. In walking Brighton throughout his life, I would always have to keep watch that he might quickly pick up anything! I am beginning to think that Enzo may have inherited that strong retrieve-anything behavior! In the first weeks, I could not let Enzo walk beside the grass, but had to keep him in the middle of the blacktop on the street to isolate his potty needs from his vacuum-cleaner eating habit. Brighton was always an eater, while Snowdon has always been a sniffer! The jury is still out with Enzo!

After having Enzo with us a couple of weeks, I began to reflect on the spirit of Brighton that may have returned in the soul of little Enzo. At times, a sudden beam of sunlight would shine through our kitchen window and leave a rainbow dot right in the middle of our kitchen floor between where Brighton and Snowdon would rest. We placed Enzo's crate horizontal to the back of a couch at a right angle to the spot Brighton loved in front of the sliding glass door to the patio deck. Several times, a sunbeam of light would shine through brightly on Enzo while he was sleeping in his crate. Likewise, a sunbeam would shine on Enzo's area when he was in the living room.

We had set up a corner in the living room as our spirit corner in honor of Brighton's memory. The silver cubed container holding his ashes was placed on the shelf in that corner under a huge, larger-than-life poster picture of Brighton looking right at us. On the floor in front of the shelving was a smaller area rug that pictured a large white dog, and that rug had been beneath Brighton's blanket the night he passed. I had put Brighton's My Pillow dog bed on top of that rug. One day, Enzo made an extra effort to pull the whole dog bed off the rug. Then he went over to the center of the rug that contained the head of the white dog. He began incessantly licking the head of the dog on the rug. I finally removed him from the dog bed and replaced the bed on the rug. Surprisingly, Enzo started barking enthusiastically at the huge poster of Brighton that was looking down on us. He put his paws on the edge of the dog bed and continued to bark at Brighton's picture. At the same time, a beam of sunlight was shining on the bed between Enzo and Brighton's poster. It seemed like such a profound sign, showing the smiling Brighton and the extension of Brighton integrated in Enzo.

Enzo was growing with puppy speed every week. He came to us at eleven weeks old, which is a little later than the usual puppy time of eight weeks. He was already larger, and his breeder had described him as big and heavy. He was getting more distinguishing characteristics. His ears were longer like Brighton's ears. His snout was longer, and his face was thinner than Snowdon's and other English crème goldens. The facial structure seemed to resemble Brighton's. I posted on Facebook a close-up of Enzo and Brighton's faces and received many comments in agreement of a similarity. I would not say that Enzo is a reincarnation of Brighton, yet, with Brighton's mother and father in Enzo's pedigree, a resemblance of any kind would not be out of line.

There is the spirit of Brighton that has returned to our lives through Enzo's B-RIGHT-ON circuit of love.

SONG INSPIRATION

"Circle of Life" (by Elton John)

Over many years, I have written over sixty personalized poems to honor retiring teachers in my school district. I would read each poem with background music at a retirement event. The poetry gave me a distinct perspective on the entire life and legacy of a teacher. The background music I selected was also designed to enhance the unique poetry theme.

I became especially attracted to the song "Circle of Life" as legacy music. This song from *The Lion King* is a beautiful tribute. Think of the lion king, and then the little lion cub, being celebrated as new life. It is like Enzo arriving as a continuation of the pedigree and spirit of Brighton! The refrain of "Circle of Life" implies a spiral of faith, hope, and love. The song's message honors the forever circuit of life with repeating seasons, birth to death, and generation to generation.

Brighton's final journey seemed to have a parallel final lap on a racing circuit, like the film *Racing in the Rain*. Then, as Brighton crossed the finish line, he arose to continue along the rainbow bridge highway. Three months later, Brighton's pedigree legacy, Enzo, was conceived. Another three months and puppy Enzo was born at Brighton's Netherlands birthplace. Then, again, in the final three-month cycle, Enzo arrived and completed the profound legacy of Brighton's forever circuit of love.

10

• •

S.O.S.

The metaphor of Circuit of Bright was meant to be the finale of this book. Yet the profound circle of life took on a deeply eternal meaning, which was far beyond anything expected in the death of Brighton and the subsequent yearlong thread woven in the tapestry with the arrival of Enzo.

Our special eleven-week-old pup arrived on September first, and his arrival had been postponed due to some medical testing scheduled for dear Pops. The results of the medical testing had not indicated any serious condition that would have caused further delay in Enzo's destiny with our family, so our new puppy arrived from the Netherlands amid joyful anticipation, and he gradually became assimilated into our home and hearts. By the end of his first week with us, Enzo and Snowdon had started to bond. Enzo's barking continued to be an unexpected addition to the COVID-19 challenge of cautionary home quarantine. Pops and I were consistently spending time at home. Enzo had not yet been ready for us to leave him in his crate without someone in the house to correct his barking while he slowly progressed in puppy training. One of my favorite photos is of Pops sitting on the back deck during a lovely summer day, holding Enzo. That was one way that Pops was able to stop Enzo's barking. Enzo had become overly attached to me, and he would immediately bark whenever I would leave.

That summer, Pops had felt more fatigue, and was being provided appropriate monitoring and guidance by combined expertise of more than one specialist. I was taking Snowdon for longer walks several times a day, and we had special concern for Pops regarding any exposure to the COVID virus. Therefore, the arrival of Enzo was a stimulating addition to our home. The excitement of a darling puppy is certainly a reason for joy and laughter, and it led to a nonstop sense of at-home entertainment. Pops and I were amused and fascinated with the sweetness of Enzo, and it was a very warm experience for Pops to hold Enzo on his lap. Pops had a jovial chuckle of humor and would always roll up his sleeves as a pragmatic problem-solver. He had often watched *The Dog Whisperer* television program and had developed with Brighton and Snowdon a wise sense of ways to control dog behaviors. Yet, barking was an issue that had inherently been more solidly ingrained in Enzo, and Pops and I knew this pup needed time and steady reinforcement with correction to gradually extinguish his tendency to bark.

Those first weeks with Enzo were a typical scenario of the new puppy dynamic, often described as similar to having a new baby in the house. Enzo was constantly under my close supervision, and he was confined to certain areas on the first floor of the house. September 21 was three weeks after Enzo had arrived. Our loving family was adapting to the monitoring of a puppy and balancing loving care with gentle discipline and training. I had developed an antibark strategy of sleeping on the couch in the first-floor family room of our home. It was important to train Enzo to be quiet throughout the night and not to disrupt Pops, who always required quiet to provide himself with needed sound sleep.

During the Sunday night of September 20, I had been sleeping downstairs with Snowdon and Enzo, as usual. Snowdon cuddled beside me, and, for some strange reason, he started to twitch his ears. This twitching had not been a problem since a previous period of time in January. On that night, Pops had a severe disturbance with an upset stomach, similar to what he had been experiencing a few times in the past month. In the morning, Pops described the severe struggle that had kept him up during the night and his consequent high level of exhaustion. He definitely had need for a day of rest. In a similar upsetting nighttime disturbance a few weeks before, Pops had rested all day to regain the sleep he had lost during the night. My concern was to give Pops the quiet rest he needed after such a rough night. I stayed downstairs with the dogs, took them for their morning walk, and made every effort to keep the house bark free and peaceful for Pops to rest. Also, I had scheduled Enzo's first outdoor appointment with our dog trainer who had known Brighton very well.

After a few hours of what had been anticipated as rest for Pops, I went upstairs to check on him. In a totally unexpected surprise, I discovered Pops had developed severe breathing. It quickly became obvious that his distress was at a point of needing medical assistance, and I made an emergency call to 911. In panic, I was shouting circumstances to 911 on the phone. I was right at his bedside when Pops suddenly experienced an acute heart failure and stopped breathing. An extensive contingent of 911 emergency responders arrived on-site within minutes, and they worked intensely to perform CPR. Tragically, after their dedicated and extensive heroic efforts, the paramedics were still unable to revive Pops, and he was gone.

Three weeks after Enzo's arrival, Pops had vanished from our lives, literally in a heartbeat. My loss of Brighton had been profound, but now our beloved Pops was also whisked over the rainbow bridge. The inspiration of Enzo's arrival had provided such joy in renewal. Now our lives had crashed in an unspeakable, traumatic devastation. A yearlong completion of the life cycle had suddenly become a haunted, broken chain that had been snapped with mortal force.

Snowdon had been in the bedroom, watching while I was calling 911, and he was a witness to Pops's traumatic passing. Snowdon had also seen Brighton right after he had passed and carries with him the memories of mourning two unplanned rainbow bridge passages. Snowdon's ears had unexpectedly started to flip when Pops was sick during the night he had died. The ear twitching then continued for weeks after Pops was gone. Was Snowdon hearing some sound from Pops, perhaps whispering that he was still with us? Whenever I relate to people the tragic circumstance of Pops's passing, Snowdon will begin to interrupt with a loud telling bark. It is almost like he is trying to give an interjecting commentary from Pops!

The week following Pops's death was a blur of tearful shock that permeated our home and the lives of all. Our son and his wife came in from their home out of state and spent a lot of time at the house trying to help plan funeral arrangements and organize final things within the context of a sudden, stunning loss. Snowdon actually became the stable anchor in the home and was such a good boy. He had been there during Pops's death, with a house full of first responders and police, and had watched and comforted me in saddened shock.

Then there was little Enzo. Luckily, he had been locked in his crate downstairs at the time Pops had passed and the first responders were invading the house. For a long time, he had continued his habit of barking and barking when he could not see me. The invasion of the strangers and police seemed to engulf him in the atmosphere of silenced shock. In fact, for over two hours, the whole house was in a stage of deadened repose, and poor Enzo was locked in his crate without me and, I'm sure, stunned as well.

There was also the unavoidable dynamic of puppy training during the week between Pops's death and the funeral. Enzo was being shifted and supervised by whoever was in the room at the time. He loved the attention and became a total pest. He took advantage of the disruption in schedule to put his potty training on hold. The house was in a high-level puppy mode of "Oh, No! Enzo!" Amid my numb sense of grief, I was also kept on alert, running to wipe up a sudden puddle or, even more aggravating, poop. Without consistency in training, Enzo was truly a handful. My son's wife came to the rescue by trying to walk Enzo up and down the block and attempting to keep him amused. Enzo was a perfect example of why people think twice before getting a puppy! He needed my 24/7 supervision, barking incessantly if he was locked in his crate and unable to see me.

People were genuinely heartbroken and shocked at Pops's sudden death and offered to help in any way possible. Doggone help came from the mom of angel Max, who I had helped in getting an English crème puppy just a year before. That new pup was named Scout, and Scout's mom came to my rescue by taking Enzo to their home to watch him for several hours each day. That compassionate caretaking allowed us to make cemetery and funeral arrangements and care for Enzo the day of the funeral. Scout's mom enjoyed having Enzo in their home for several days for longer periods of time. Scout loved having Enzo around and they played for hours, where Scout would act visibly sad when Enzo left. Best buddies, Enzo and Scout's friendship became one of the many graces that occurred during such a tragic time.

Losing Pops left me in stunned grief, and I kept repeating, "What in the world happened?" It was so fast, so final, so unexpected. The whole family was engulfed in grief, plus haunted and declaring, "It makes no sense." It was the circle of a year. Brighton was diagnosed on September 5. Just one year later on September I marked the arrival of Brighton's descendent, Enzo. The year's circuit had closed from sadness to new joy. Then, three weeks later, a profound, tragic death fractured the circuit of love. Hope again needed to be replaced by faith.

It was nine months from the time that Brighton passed on December 9, to Pops's daunting death on September 21. One spiritually reflective friend commented, "It almost seemed that dealing with the grief of Brighton had been a training period for the unexpected passing of Pops."

So many questions haunted me. Was the nine months from Brighton's death to the death of Pops like a pregnancy or gestation in integrating a spiritual experience and belief in the afterlife? Is Enzo, in spirit, the DNA manifestation of Brighton? If I believed that Brighton's spirit is truly alive, then the death of Pops is God's way of manifesting for me the mystery of afterlife. Brighton's spirit seems to permeate the life of little Enzo. The spirit of Pops seems to speak in sudden, unwarranted barking from his beloved Snowdon.

Then I have interpreted messages, like the lyrics of "Spanish Eyes." The video had shown a Spanish gentleman leading the golden horse to dance with the Flamenco lady. The horse seemed to be a metaphor for Brighton, and the Flamenco dancer a symbol for me. Now it seemed that the Spanish gentleman was Pops! During the song, both the man and the horse exit. Then they return with the horse now in angelic white and in close union with the Spanish gentleman. The horse returning seemed to be a symbol of Brighton in angelic form. Yet there was no clue, until now, that the Spanish gentleman who was returning was also Pops in his angel form. Both of them had left, but then they returned once again to dance with me. I am their forever lady!

The whole passing of Pops made no sense, as his medical situation had been under control, and we had just met at length with the specialist four days before. The only thing that could make sense in this mystery was that it was time for Pops to transition, and that his spirit is in the afterlife. Just like Brighton, our loved ones who leave us must still have life in spirit and must be with us in heavenly form! Was my dual experience of profound loss and grief an inspiration to use my gift of words to inspire others to have faith in the afterlife? What would make sense? Perhaps God provided this experience of such profound loss because He knew it could be inspired as an instrument in His message of eternal life. Was I recruited into the boot camp of loss and grief as an instrument to actualize a gift of the Word? I feel a profound message in the song lyric, "I've seen the light." Does that refer to afterlife? Seems to fit!

If I had a previous life of a Spanish lady, then perhaps Pops and I also shared a previous life. Pops had been a man with a profound and impressive historical connection. He had always read and talked of heroes, like the Knights of the Round Table,

Indiana Jones, and General George Patton. Before his death, Pops had been doing in-depth reading about the Templars. He seemed the archetype of El Cid, and with me as his princess, perhaps we lived a romantic past in the Middle Ages!

It is profound that Brighton remains as my heart dog, even a year after he is gone. With the direct experience of the sudden death of Pops, both my heart dog and my soul mate have sadly vanished from my everyday life. Yet, they are not gone. In one sense, Pops is my ancient soulmate hero who transcends the ages. He is still in our home through Snowdon and is forever embedded as part of my heart. He is truly the mate of my soul!

Pops's passing in September put a new circuit into gear. They say grief takes a year of going through every annual event without the loved one. At fifteen months, Enzo will be fully grown and mature. Hopefully I will feel some peace with Brighton and Pops in the afterlife. Perhaps my life's destiny will also have been sealed with a mature inspiration that I can be a message of faith for others. The title of this book is *Brighton Mourning,* and it conveys the narrative of the experience of loss and navigating the rapids of grief. The final metaphor of mourning is:

Mourning the soul of night
Brighton in morning light

SOS – Spirit of Soul

Just as there were signs of the afterlife appearing after Brighton passed, I now craved signs from Pops, who had so suddenly left our life. Snowdon somehow seemed to be the messenger for Pops.

At times, Snowdon exhibited strange behaviors, when it could almost be seen as subtle signs of Pops's spirit.

A very unusual incident occurred the week before Thanksgiving, when our son and his wife arrived from out of town for an early holiday visit. When they entered the house, Snowdon was exuberant! It seemed he was the happiest he had been since their previous visit weeks after the funeral. When my son entered the room, Snowdon would bark and bark nonstop. In trying to quiet Snowdon, I thought, *That's Pops! Snowdon is talking for Pops and is so thrilled to have our son back at home.*

That is exactly how Pops would react to having our dear son walk in the door. It seemed that, through Snowdon, Pops was trying to show his excitement for his son's return home!

The evening of their arrival, my son and his wife left for an hour. At that time, I noticed that the stainless-steel kitchen sink needed to be polished and took an SOS box out of the cabinet below the sink, removing one SOS pad. A load of clothes was in the dryer, so I quickly went down into the basement to fold the clothes. Enzo was locked in his crate, and Snowdon was in his crate with the door open, finishing his dinner. Snowdon was always such a good boy and had freedom on the first floor, while Enzo was not yet trustworthy enough to leave alone outside his crate.

After quickly folding the clothes, I came up the stairs from the basement and strolled back into the kitchen. As I approached the sink, Snowdon uncharacteristically dashed past. I was very surprised and realized Snowdon had something in his mouth. I ran, grabbed his head, and quickly pried open his jaw, as he fought to protect his hidden surprise. Low and behold, in his mouth was the shredded half of a new blue dry SOS pad! I needed to act quickly! I grabbed a dishcloth to wet profusely, chased Snowdon into the next room, as he assertively dodged being attacked. I finally caught him, put the cloth in his mouth, and attempted to wipe out the bright-blue SOS powder and pieces of shredded steel wool.

Once I had wiped Snowdon's mouth as best as possible, I returned to the sink. On the floor in front of the sink was less than a half piece of blue SOS pad, sitting in a small area of blue SOS pad dust. That meant that Snowdon had eaten nearly half of an SOS pad! I freaked out and ran into the back room to retrieve a plastic bag that was an emergency kit ready to induce vomiting. I quickly reviewed the instructions typed on a sheet in large print. It involved using the large dropper to squirt hydrogen peroxide into Snowdon's mouth. I loaded the dropper and began to chase Snowdon, who quickly kept escaping my hold. Finally, I was able to get a tiny squirt in his mouth, and then had to give up!

In my dog-owner's mind, I rationalized that dogs often eat things they shouldn't. I recalled endless stories of dogs pooping out socks, gloves, and various other ingested items. By the same token, the blue powder was alarming, and I did not know if it was highly toxic. My mind had been so hypervigilant in taking care of Brighton until the end. For months, I had worried about Pops's health issues, which eventually did lead to his death. My catastrophic mindset was primed for the worst-case scenario, and that reality could actually be death.

Thankfully, the vet clinic was still open, and I called to immediately explain the emergency situation. A nurse put me on hold to consult Snowdon's vet and returned with instructions:

"Give Snowdon three pieces of bread, and do not induce vomiting. The vomiting up of the steel wool could cause damage to his throat. The bread should bond to the steel wool and cushion it in a softer mass as it moves through his digestive system."

So, there I was, giving Snowdon bread, which normally he is never allowed to eat. Boy, was he having a good time! He had to be monitored all night to see if there were any symptoms of toxic distress. As it turned out, Snowdon did not experience any digestive issues from swallowing the steel wool. By his third poop the following day, it had moved through his stomach and intestines. He produced a delightful black turd of poop that was bound together with a pasty fiber that was firm and "wiry." Whew! It was a definite relief from one of those doggone unexpected mishaps that are a legendary part of having a golden retriever.

What really was puzzling was the whole incident of Snowdon ingesting the S.O.S. pad to begin with. This was absolutely uncharacteristic of him. In the past years he had matured tremendously, and this was beyond his normal behavior. Whenever something strange happens that is so uncanny and out of the norm, it is a clue to stop and think about whether this is a case of "coincidence is God's way of remaining anonymous." That type of occurrence is often given the term "synchronicity," a concept connected with the psychologist Carl Gustave Jung.

I reflected on this incident with Snowdon and thought about a possible message. How ironic that it was an S.O.S. pad! S.O.S. is a term used as a signal to alert authorities about an emergency. Since I had suspected that Snowdon might be barking as a signal from Pops, I wondered if Snowdon's temptation to take the S.O.S. pad was also a signal of alert. Was it a message to not take

Snowdon for granted, or was Snowdon giving a signal that he felt the need for attention? Was it, in some way, a signal from Pops to alert us that he was there, watching over us? I could only ponder that somehow it was Pops using Snowdon as a messenger to get our attention!

The passing of Brighton and Pops left a profound void in my heart and soul. Truly, the sound of silence! Perhaps that is the message of faith that sustains me through the anguish of grief in the loss of my heart dog followed by the shocking loss of my soul mate of over fifty years. S.O.S. is a symbol of alert! Was it also a SOS – Sign of Spirit?

Snowdon's full pedigree name is Polar Express of the Morning Valley. It was ironic that *The Polar Express* was one of Pops's absolute favorite films. He loved Christmas so much. In *The Polar Express*, the innocent and naïve young boy looks a lot like Pops did as a kid. The boy is transported by train to the North Pole and sees the real Santa Claus. Yet, the profound message of the movie is locked within the power of a bell. The bell will only ring for those who *believe*! For others who do not believe in Santa, the bell is silent. Dear Pops was an adult who never stopped believing in the SOS – Spirit of Santa! S.O.S again! Truly, the bell always rang for him! When Brighton crossed over the rainbow bridge, Pops joined me in faith, believing that Brighton was still with us in spirit. Together, we kept watch to recognize signs of Brighton from the afterlife.

The grief between Brighton's passing and the sudden passage of Pops was a time when our whole family embraced the faith to *believe* in life everlasting. We felt Brighton's soul was alive in our home and in our hearts. The spirit corner in our living room was always graced with fresh white flowers. It was important for Brighton to know we welcomed his spirit, and that we encouraged him to gladly return to us in the form of light beams, rainbow dots, and the daily chirping of a red cardinal.

Is it possible that the nine months of grief we endured after Brighton's loss was a spiritual training ground for the coming of an even more-profound loss? Pops transitioned so abruptly to the other side, just three weeks after Enzo arrived in our lives. Enzo was our metaphor for the reincarnation of the spirit of Brighton! With Enzo, we had survived Brighton's transition to spirit as a family, and we believed. Now, a sudden and shocking death of our Pops was a final test of my faith! Do I truly believe? Can I believe that Brighton is here with us in the SOS – Sign of Spirit in Enzo? If so, then I can believe and affirm that the circuit of love continues with beloved Pops in his SOS – Sign of Spirit (or SOS – Spirit of Santa)!

Brighton's story has been a journey of faith in life everlasting and a personal boot camp to truly believe. I had survived and graduated from the grief of the boot camp of loss of Brighton. Now I am gradually sprouting wings of faith in the certainty that Pops is still with me! The journey has been guided by Snowdon, our own Polar Express. With signs from Snowdon and Enzo, our home is blessed with the sign of spirit in Brighton and Pops. Our hearts are surrounded by another S.O.S., the Serenity of Solitude. We have the SOS – Spirit of Soul that blesses us with the grace of everlasting life and love. Pops believed, and in his honor, I delicately placed a bell in his pocket in the casket. I know he can hear the bell ring, and his voice resounds with us forever as belief in the S.O.S. Spirit of Santa.

SONG INSPIRATION

"The Sound of Silence" (by Simon & Garfunkel)

S.O.S. connects with one song that had appeared to me several times during Brighton's final journey. There were haunting versions of the song "Sound of Silence," sung by an acapella group called Pentatonix and a haunting version by the recording artist named Disturbed. The message of that classic 1960s song launches a desperate crawl through the dark. That was a mystery that had been haunting me in Brighton's passage and then with the sudden death of Pops.

The lyrics of "Sound of Silence" pervade the solitude journey of loss, broken only by a slim hint of bright. Silence is the dark language of death. Grief brings with it restless dreams and memories of moments now lost and the reality of the profound sense of being alone. Sometimes along the path of grief, our eyes stare longingly for a glimpse or glimmer of hope. We feel permeated by the nagging winter chill of a perpetually rainy day. Alone in a crowd, no syllable seems allowed. Songs just haunt our memories, muffled by thick masks for all. Solitude engulfs the grief, surrounded by a yearning for relief, craving whispers that might barely echo in a deep well of breathless serenity. All we hear in our memories is the haunting sign of spirit … and perhaps the bell.

11

....

"It's Me"

There was an S.O.S. sound of silence that was living within my special angel, Pops, and his essence permeated the entire journey of *Brighton Mourning*. Chapter 1 establishes the grief experiences of losing so many pet bunnies to their shorter natural lifespans. In the shadows of repeated loss was the silent support from Pops. There were times when he came home from work to find trauma and tears and the overwhelming, shocking discovery of a bunny that suddenly and mysteriously died. He was there in the lovely condo in Hawaii when word came by phone from the vet at home that the bunny left in the vet hospital's care had passed. A highly anticipated Hawaii trip in paradise became shrouded in a cloud of loss through unexpressed pet grief.

The last bunny died soon after I had completed a year of cancer treatment. Pops was an eyewitness to me standing in the kitchen with the final squeal of my precious Thumpy expiring in my arms. What can a man do to comfort the screaming reaction to death that was so intensely reverberating across the room? Even a strong heroic knight like Lancelot can only feel silent and helpless in the desire to rescue the anguish of a sobbing Guinevere. The sound of silence of the stoic man could only permeate the castle with the cold damp void in the empty creep of grief.

Throughout the journey of *Brighton Mourning*, there is mention of Pops, but he is in the background. Like an intravenous drip, he is silently diffusing sadness and loss. Pops was a major factor in the decision against Brighton's surgery after consultation with the veterinary specialty hospital regarding the spleen tumor diagnosis. In fact, the intense struggle with the surgery decision created tremendous discord in our relationship. Pops also saw the reality that declining surgery was best for Brighton. He also felt tremendous hurt in being excluded from my hasty decision without his consult. Pops had been reconsidering that it was more loving to Brighton to give him the gift of quiet days in hospice in this impending final journey. In a conciliatory reflection after the decision, Pops even expressed that surgery was more of a concern for our needs and not for Brighton's peaceful passage. I readily admit it is a natural tendency for humans to do everything to avoid death. Once we had reached an agreement on the final decision favoring hospice over surgery, Pops manifested an incredible amount of strength and wisdom. He was truly the silent partner in the three months leading to the inevitable day of Brighton crossing the rainbow bridge.

After the hospice prognosis, Pops became the silent copilot of peace, always in the shadows, ready to be called upon for support. Brighton had become extremely fond of Pops during the three-year period when I was limited in my ability to walk due to subsequent hip- and knee-replacement surgeries. Pops had always loved to travel and was like a global citizen. Yet, with my long period of surgeries and the need to use a cane, Pops heroically took over walking the dogs throughout the cold and snowy days of winter, which included struggling to get boots on their feet for each walk. He was confined to being home for us, with his pervasive sense of loyalty that was his lifelong trademark of a truly loving, faithful husband and father.

Brighton loved the way Pops always had kibble in his pocket, and Brighton became a master of manipulation in refusing to get up or move unless Pops gave him a kibble treat. Pops didn't really mind. In fact, leaving the house, Pops would always remember to toss a few pieces of kibble on the ottoman for Brighton to treasure upon return. Pops, in fact, was the man in charge of food in the house, and Brighton and Snowdon knew it. In the last months of Brighton's life, I had finally recovered and was in charge of the walks. Pops was in charge of morning and evening meals that waited for the boys as soon as they came in from their early potty breaks with me. Pops took pride in his kibble "chief chef" job, as he knew how much the boys treasured their food. Brighton was especially food-driven, and Pops would call him the "beggar man."

From Brighton's diagnosis around Labor Day, until his passing the second week in December, either Pops or I stayed home almost all the time. It was worrisome to leave Brighton home alone, as he would start barking for no reason. Also, we worried that he might sometimes leave an unexpected poop as he walked through the house. Pops found that when Brighton barked, it would help if he came close so Brighton could see him. Pops was always on poop alert, signaling for me to come running with paper towels for my jiffy cleanup routine. Pops often wanted me to go out with him for a meal or an errand, but he adjusted his life to limit plans so both of us would not need to be out of the house.

The middle of October was usually a time for celebration, as within nine days it was Pops's birthday, as well as our wedding anniversary. Yet that fateful fall became the final October for Brighton and the unexpected final birthday for Pops. Brighton had a serious decline right during that time in October. Pops and I rushed him to the vet, so afraid and panic-stricken that it was time for him to be put to sleep. Pops sat with us in the exam room stoically. Dr. P. recognized that the tumor had not ruptured, and through an adjustment in meds, the crisis was diverted and, in a few days, turned around.

It was also Brighton's gift to Pops to rally in October. It would have been a sad remembrance if his death had also become connected with Pops's last yearly birthday celebration. Likewise, this was our last wedding anniversary together. Our anniversary gift became Brighton's revival, where we could celebrate and go out for dinner. It was also a gift of renewed hope for us that he might make it through a full three-month survival and possibly be with us for Thanksgiving and Christmas.

Throughout the three months of fall, Brighton was still able to walk slowly around the block, and Pops expressed such genuine compassion for his aging beggar man. There were many times when Pops would say to Brighton that he felt sorry for him and genuinely did understand. Pops had experienced some health issues starting that summer, and he could identify with Brighton as to feeling they were both in a slowing-down process. It is recognized that dogs do not show they are in pain or discomfort, as it is part of their survival instinct. Pops was the same way. It would be unlike him to express discomfort or concern about any compromised health. Brighton and Pops had truly bonded as my Yoda pair.

Pops and our son also unfortunately understood that we could not take our usual out-of-town trip to visit our son in Texas for Thanksgiving. Instead, Pops made a reservation at a nice local restaurant for us to get out for a brief time to celebrate with a holiday turkey dinner buffet. It was a lonesome-yet-necessary holiday adjustment, where our conversations were reflective, as there wasn't a lot we had to say.

Pops always enjoyed eating at nice restaurants and tried to remain festive in his dinner talk. He said, "I really like this restaurant. It's upscale, and they do a good job. The turkey is great, and I love the mashed potatoes and dressing. They have a nice salad. The little pieces of dessert are a good idea, and I like the brownies."

It is important for me to have others know the Pops who was our silent support, with such fatherly love for Brighton and Snowdon—who he insisted on calling "Snowman." Even at elaborate buffet meals, he was a simple meat-and-potatoes kind of guy. He especially loved chocolate chip cookies and brownies, and he could live on a good hamburger with only ketchup.

Our Thanksgiving that year would not have been celebrated any other way than honoring Brighton over going out of town for a special family holiday. Pops had the heart of a father his whole life, and Brighton was the child who especially needed him that year. What is so profoundly sad and emotionally gut-wrenching for me and my son is that we never realized it would be the last family Thanksgiving for both Brighton and Pops.

The final days of Brighton's journey were becoming more evident. The house would become very quiet while Dr. M. would come and give Brighton his weekly acupuncture treatment. Pops would sit at the computer and silently watch out of the corner of his eye. He would almost wince in painful empathy with the long needles being placed strategically in Brighton's body. Pops never understood whether that strange therapy was helpful. Yet, he never complained about the added expense of Dr. M.'s home visits. Pops's silent compassion and caring always loomed as love in the shadows of everything I tried to do. He was always covert in his quiet strength and love. On the other hand, I was always commenting and demonstrating overt strategies to keep Brighton comfortable. We were both also doing our best to entertain Snowdon, who was learning not to pester and be a wondering witness.

Two nights before Brighton passed, Pops and I were scheduled to attend a special Christmas party hosted by dear friends who had lost their golden angel, Benson, a few years before. Brighton was definitely slipping and unable to move by himself, and there was no way I would be able to attend. Pops went to the event alone, as it was held only five minutes from our home. Once again, he was losing valued time with me in honoring his incredible support and loyalty to Brighton.

On the evening of Brighton's last night, Pops bravely held Brighton's head while I inhaled a huge breath of courage before injecting Brighton with the emergency syringe containing a tranquilizer and pain killer. It was so hard for Pops to watch, as he always had anxiety about injections for himself. Pops had to reach into the reserve of his own stoic medical apprehension and courageously become a solid support for my brave and anguish-stricken first attempt at administering an injection.

The morning after Brighton passed, Pops took on the courageous man's role of assisting Dr. M. in carrying Brighton's body to the SUV. In somber silence, Pops transported Brighton's shrouded body to the animal cemetery for cremation, with me holding on to Snowdon in the back seat. It was so hard for Pops to wrap his big arms around me at the cemetery visitation room. He had to embrace the experience that my tears wouldn't stop and cushion the shaking anguish that was permeating my being. Pops also was holding on to Snowdon and keeping him calm, while he gave me as much time as I needed to reverently give Brighton my final good-bye touches. A week later, Pops again became the strength that courageously stayed with me the entire time that Brighton's body was cremated. He watched me sob for almost two hours straight, barely said a word, and never rushed to pull me away. His gift of patience and understanding was his unforgettable true sound of silence.

During the holidays following Brighton's passage, I was emotionally drained and unable to decorate our traditional, elaborate, large Christmas tree. It was a smaller, delicate gold tree that Pops accepted as a somber symbol for Christmas, never knowing it was going to be his last Christmas tree as well. Pops was the epitome of Christmas and had the spirit of Santa Claus. It was a time when he would "Brighton" our whole family. Pops's life as a child was very similar to the classic film *A Christmas Story,* and there were touching similarities between his boyhood and that of the boy in the starring role of Ralphie. When the more recent movie *The Polar Express* was released, Pops was fascinated with that story, and I would find him watching it several times during the holiday season. *The Polar Express* became very symbolic, as Pops always integrated the spirit of Santa and never stopped hearing the bell of Santa Claus.

The months following the holidays were serene and found Pops hearing me wistfully relating inspired tales of sensing Brighton's afterlife spirit. There would be visits in the form of rainbow dots and the daily chirp of a cardinal. Every day, I would mention some belief in a little sign that Brighton's spirit was still with us. It appeared in slow, drip-by-drip intravenous granules of faith, building a deeper belief in the afterlife. At the same time, Pops had developed a cardiac condition that needed more attention. In February, we became fearful that either Pops or I were at a dangerous risk for becoming sick with the COVID-19 virus. Like everyone else, our house became a quarantine refuge amid a pandemic.

Brighton's passage became a prelude to the months that haunted both Pops and me. It was also felt by Snowdon, as he exhibited a sadness at the of loss of his lifelong buddy, Brighton. We lost the certainty of our own health by early February. Our dog walks with Snowdon became strolls of social distancing and the little joys of a cardinal chirping every day. Pops and I had not only lost Brighton but also our ability to socially connect with others who might help us work through the grief that came in losing a cherished angel dog.

Somewhere in the continuing struggle, I began to search for a beam of hope and found it in the anticipated arrival of Enzo. Dear Pops had the reaction of many who have gone through the pain of losing a dog. He did not want to get another dog. Yet for me, there was hope for the addition of a new pup from Brighton's heritage pedigree in his Netherlands breeder. It would help me to heal from the loss and hopefully bring back the youthful spirit that had also disappeared in Snowdon.

After much convincing, Pops finally acquiesced to getting the puppy when he was born in June. Pops loved auto racing his whole life, and it was appealing that I wanted to name the pup Enzo, after Enzo Ferrari. Pops had always been fond of the Morning Valley Kennel as the birthplace of Brighton and Snowdon. He often affectionately recalled our visit to Morning Valley in the Netherlands the year Snowdon was born and even said more than once that he'd like to visit there again.

Enzo was born on June 10, and all that summer he was a growing pup in the Netherlands while we were trapped in fear and the ever-present threat of COVID-19. Pictures of Enzo and his litter mates were being posted on the Morning Valley website, and that became the bright spot of our confined summer. Pops had been a world traveler his whole career, with anticipation of an international trip each summer. Therefore, he especially felt the trapped frustration of the pandemic. Plus, there had been some additional health issues in January, and they had become a source of ongoing monitoring and treatment. The cloud that came with Brighton's passage never seemed to lift. Despite growing optimism throughout the country, the pandemic burden also refused to dissipate.

Pops and I shared a renewed glimmer of encouragement with

the arrival of Enzo on September 1. Enzo was almost twelve weeks old, and we had arranged with the breeder in the Netherlands to keep him there a couple of extra weeks. Pops, in the meantime, had completed some diagnostic testing at the hospital. The test results did not indicate that Pops had anything of serious concern. So, Enzo was shipped from Amsterdam as scheduled.

It had been a questionable decision to bring Enzo into our lives. Yet, from my brokenhearted perspective, it seemed a key to my healing the sense of loss in lonesome Snowdon. Enzo arrived, and I committed to a herculean effort of training the new pup. Any initial stress of a barking puppy was balanced by the enriching sense of joy that only holding a puppy can bring. I became tenacious in attempting to alleviate Enzo's tendency to bark whenever I was out of sight. I also needed to give Snowdon the attention he needed in his daily walks. Pops was such a good sport. He made such an effort to amuse and calm Enzo while I would take Snowdon for his treasured alone-time strolls.

Enzo's barking became much more of a puppy challenge than I anticipated. We had strategies to quell it while Enzo was in sight. Yet, if I would leave Enzo in his crate alone, the continuous barking was resistant to some of the common puppy training tricks of the trade. At times, I would feel it necessary to put Enzo in the large SUV crate and just take him with me, as Enzo traveled quietly during rides in the car.

On the seventeenth day after Enzo's arrival, Pops had a doctor's appointment with the specialist to go over the hospital test results. With the pandemic, it was a regulation for only the patient to go into the doctor's office. I put Enzo in the crate in the SUV, and Pops drove to the doctor's office building. We had made the arrangement that as soon as the doctor would enter the examination room, Pops would phone me. Pops explained to the doctor that I was outside in the SUV with our new barking puppy. Throughout the half-hour discussion with the doctor, Enzo was perfectly quiet, and I was fully able to participate by phone in the entire meeting. It again provided no deep concern about a serious medical situation. Pops felt the meeting with the doctor went well, ending with a plan to get a new series of blood tests the following Monday.

The uneventful doctor's appointment was on Thursday, and the following weekend, Pops continued to experience his feelings of chronic fatigue, but nothing else changed. Yet, three days later, Pops unexpectedly experienced a difficult night, and midday on Monday, he suffered an acute attack of heart failure. Our Pops quickly passed away at home with me calling 911, with first responders just minutes away and Snowdon in the room watching in stunned silence.

Throughout that final weekend, we had not had any deep concern about a worsening, much less mortal, condition with Pops until late Sunday night. Pops was always the silent hero who would endure discomfort. Just like Brighton, he would not let on to any discomfort or pain. That night, not even Pops had any idea that a recurrence of intestinal distress would thrust him into his rapid trajectory to the rainbow bridge.

Throughout the days after Pops's tragic passing, the expressions of sorrow and shock were overwhelming and so profound. Descriptions like "good man, kind, friendly, helpful, jovial, caring, and loyal" were woven into cards with written notes and a truly heartbreaking eulogy written by his only son. We were able to have a modified, socially distanced funeral mass for him, which was a grace. Pops was the best dad in the world, and the anguish at this sudden, tragic loss was impossible to fully bear. Our son created a fifteen-day series of remembrance writings that he dedicated to Pops for consecutive days on Facebook. His reflection about Pops and the dogs is shared at the end of this chapter.

This book has the title of *Brighton Mourning,* and it is a touching true story of the profound mourning that transcends the understanding of many who have also felt the deep grief in loss. This narrative about Brighton is written in my voice. Yet, the profound sense of unconditional love and grief must also be honored in the sound of silence that was Pops's way of caring deeply and that made him at a loss for words.

Most pet grief posts seen on Facebook are in the voices of grief from females who are feeling a sense of the loss of a child. Yet, Pops's perspective is equally as deep. There is anguish woven within the silence that is often the stereotyped expectation of men. They hold back tears, and their spoken words are concise. The depth of heartbreak of those on the sidelines may be hidden and sadly overlooked. To the readers on this journey through mourning, please remember Pops. Honor the silent support and patience of others who may not feel personal or cultural permission to express their grief. They have also been courageous knights in shining armor who have stood in the wings. They also silently suffer as the curtain of grief drops tragically on them.

This book, *Brighton Mourning,* is dedicated to my knight in shining armor, my El Cid. Pops is the hero of my heart. Now Pops and Brighton are together, as heart mate and soul mate—angels faithfully bound forever as mine. Pops was really a simple, genuine

Polar Express little boy and a man of few words. It is ironic that his last words to me were a simple response, "It's me."

A Loving Son's Fifteen-Days Remembrance of Pops
Saturday—October 10, Day Twelve

The Dog Whisperer

As a young boy, while some had cats, most of my friends had dogs, and dogs were the primary pet kids in my neighborhood wanted. I was no different. But, I learned early on that, with my Dad's allergies, having a dog was not going to happen. When we would go over to my grandparents' house, the hair and dander from their dog would cause my Dad's allergies to act-up, and he was miserable. My Mom also wanted to have a dog, and, after some negotiation, my Mom and I decided that having a rabbit as a pet would be a reasonable compromise.

They were small, could be confined to a portion of the house, and my Dad would not have to deal with hair and dander. So, for many years, my Mom and I took care of one or two rabbits at a time, while my Dad tolerated them in the house, without expressing a lick of interest in caring for them.

When my Mom and Dad moved to their current home, unbeknownst to me, they decided to get a dog. Not a small, rabbit-size dog. Oh no, they went "all-in" and bought a white golden retriever. Brighton is what my Mom named him, and he became part of the family. When I found out they bought Brighton, I had to sit down for a minute, because I never thought my Dad would live with a dog. When we came and visited them, and I watched him with the dog, I would sometimes ask Dad, "Who are you and what have you done with my father?" Little did I know that this change was only the beginning.

About four years later, my Mom and Dad decided to add a second dog, another white golden retriever. So, if you're keeping score at home, this is a man who could not stand to be in a room with one dog while I was growing up, and now had two(!) seventy-pound white golden retrievers in the house. The second dog my Mom named Snowdon, to which my Dad and I said, "Huh?" Well, my Dad said forget that, and he called him Snowman. Problem solved. My Dad took to "the Snowman" and became the dog whisperer with him. He would feed him treats, play with him, have him sit on his lap, marvel at how much of an active dog he was by nicknaming him "the loon," and laugh hysterically at how this dog would entertain and enlighten their lives. When Snowman would attack Brighton, Dad would call him "Cato" (Pink Panther reference). When My Dad traveled, he would talk to Mom first, then talk through the phone to Snowman, who would bark in response. My Dad would leave voicemail messages, bellowing SNOWMAN! on the recorder for all to hear. Again, who are you and what have you done with my father?!?!

Dad came to love both dogs. As Brighton got older, Dad would walk him and feel sadness that he was struggling and becoming less mobile, while watching Snowman continue to be the "loon." Dad would pet them, have them sit with him on the couch, carry them into the back of the SUV if they needed to go to the vet, have them join him on the outside porch during his last year, and consistently tempt them with treats. He mellowed incredibly while being the father of these dogs, and while he would complain about the hair—his clothes would always have a loving coating of white dog hair—they added happiness and joy into his life. I think they added a sense of play while providing unconditional love. No matter how bad of a day he had, no matter what was going on in the world, and

no matter what challenge he was facing, these dogs loved him and would "Brighton" his day. Some of the best pictures and memories we have in the last few years are with my Dad and the dogs, and I have no doubt he is still whispering to "the Snowman."
—*James Stone*

SONG INSPIRATION

"Faithfully" (by Journey)

A theme emerged in this book beginning in chapter 4. When it became inevitable that Brighton was in his final passage, there was a need to let go of hope and transcend to a higher power of faith that his final days were in God's hands.

Faith became an even greater key word after Brighton passed. I had to maintain faith that there is an afterlife and that Brighton's spirit was still with me. He was forever in my heart. The message of faith grew exponentially when Pops suddenly died. I had faith that Brighton's destiny was in the hands of a higher power and that he had transitioned over the rainbow bridge. Now, it was necessary to also have faith that Pops had transitioned over the bridge and was in heaven with Brighton.

The song "Faithfully" has long been a special song with a message for over fifty years of my life married to Pops. He had been a corporate businessman and was a professional in global logistics. It led to frequent business travel both in the United States as well as in other parts of the world. Often, he would be getting ready to leave home on Sunday nights and catch a limo for the airport early on Monday morning. It was ironic that his last full night on Earth was also a Sunday night. He died just after one o'clock on Monday afternoon. Brighton also had his last full day of life on earth on a Sunday, and he passed early Monday morning, around two o'clock. Sundays are still sad for me.

The song "Faithfully" is about a musician who is on the road, yet no matter where he is, there remains a faithful connection with his love. There is a line in the song about being on the road, on a travel circuit. Pops would often travel an entire week. When he was in Europe or Asia, it would often be two weeks before he'd return home. Yet, he always kept in touch by phone and email or text, and I would follow his flights to see that he had landed safely. We were far apart, yet always together in heart. When he passed, my soul continued its lifelong training that our heart connection was still there, and it always will be. It remains a long-distance connection, just like the message in "Faithfully."

It is the mood and message in the song "Faithfully" that helped to sustain me in Brighton's passage. I now continue the experience of being apart yet together. With both Pops and Brighton now across the rainbow bridge, it is faith that sustains me. I am left behind as the faithful mom and widow. I feel they are on the next part of their forever journey. It is as though they are vacationing at an ultimate resort that is "heavenly." Just as when I traveled and left Brighton behind, or when Pops traveled and left me behind, we were always connected in heart and soul. So it is now and forever in the divine journey that we are sustained by the faithful promise of us reuniting again. Someday, we will suddenly catch sight of each other in wonder and say our simple, forever love message, "It's me."

12

• •

B-RIGHT-ON

There are many references to the "rainbow bridge" in the passing of dogs. This phrase originated in a poem that became a metaphor for the death of pets. In chapter 7, I had an animal communicator make contact with Brighton's spirit in the afterlife. Brighton reported being happy and appeared young and lively. He had taken on the role of greeting others crossing the bridge and showing them which way to go. It seemed quite fitting in Brighton's afterlife that he had become a teacher.

The original plan for *Brighton Mourning* called for ten chapters. Its conclusion, at that time, was planned with no suspicion that Pops would be joining Brighton over the rainbow bridge just three weeks after Enzo's arrival. Once Pops died, I was thrown into deep and profound thoughts about afterlife.

Brighton had died peacefully on his own terms at home, and I imagined that he was being guided by angels and gracefully gliding over the rainbow bridge. It is easy to have a vision of a group of golden retrievers welcoming him. That would include his mama, Lourdes, and papa, Nielson. Then I thought of the many other fur angels who were part of the support system along Brighton's journey. I can see angels Benson and Max welcoming Brighton and filling him in on the lay of the land in heaven. After a few days of sniffing around on heavenly pathways and romping over the verdant hills, I then envisioned Brighton being reviewed by the Master Shepherd. I can see Brighton sitting in his "good boy" position, wagging his tail in awe of the feelings of divine love that now permeated his spirit.

The Master Shepherd would have summarized Brighton's life in terms of his "good boy" reputation. I think God would readily agree that Brighton's lifelong purpose was to "brighton the lives of others" and to "B-Right-On." He was a perfect role model for becoming part of the corps of the rainbow bridge welcoming committee, with the honored title of teacher. He warmly greets others crossing the rainbow bridge. He guides them through the heavenly landscape to the area that would be a designated field for each new angel. Brighton was assigned the teacher role in heaven because he had lived that during his life on earth. He was the ultimate B-right-on role model.

From the time Brighton assumed his role as teacher in the rainbow bridge world, he also diligently watched over the lives of Pops and Snowdon and me. He was an invisible witness to my tearful moments and to Pops's sense of loss. Pops and I had been with Brighton every moment during cremation, where we were able to bear witness to his physical body becoming spirit amid an eternal flame. The urn that holds his ashes had Brighton's name and date and photos inserted on each side of the cube. The whole corner of the living room where he was when he transitioned became an altar in his honor and made him feel that his spirit is still at home with Pops, Snowdon, Enzo, and me.

The animal communicator's connection to Brighton was approximately four months after he died. Brighton told the animal communicator that he liked the book I had written about his life. He liked the title *Brighton Morning: Doggone Wags of Wisdom to B-RIGHT-ON*. Brighton related how he loved me and appreciated everything that I had done to keep his spirit alive and well in his earthly home. I had collected a small library of books about the animal afterlife and learned to watch for typical signs to welcome Brighton's intermittent spirit visits.

At the same time, the COVID-19 pandemic had fully thrown our world into quarantine and isolation. Pops needed increased care for a medical issue that had developed after Brighton had passed. Then, when Pops tragically passed, my vision of Brighton's spirit became a duel welcoming of Pops with Brighton. Brighton and Pops both passed on at home in their own time. It seemed like Pops was joining Brighton, who was waiting for him. What would be the chances that they would both embark on their journey over the rainbow bridge from the same home and on the same day of the week?

My grieving heart formed a magical vision of Brighton across the rainbow bridge welcoming others. Then, suddenly, just nine months after he had settled into his rainbow teacher role, I had to envision that Brighton was waiting across the threshold to welcome his beloved Pops! It brings such a comforting smile to imagine Pops crossing the rainbow bridge and Brighton there, woofing, wagging his tail, and jumping for joy in a heavenly reunion. I am sure the first thing Brighton would have done was to sniff at Pops's pants pocket to beg for his beloved kibble treats! I can only imagine that Pops, likewise, would have immediately reached in his pocket to treat his beloved beggar man! Now, it is profound to imagine them strolling around the rainbow roadways of heaven and finding the perfect spot on a bench to sit together and have Pops stroke Brighton's exquisite fur!

The poem "The Rainbow Bridge," has become a comforting metaphor for the passage of death as a transition across a threshold that is like a bridge between life on earth and the afterlife in heaven. In books and artist renditions, the image of the rainbow bridge and heaven are often represented by a beautiful pastoral scene where animals can run freely across hills and meadows of flowers that are the most beautiful representations of Mother Nature.

If one enters a search on Google for images with the subject "rainbow bridge," many similar pictures will appear. A colorful bridge often crosses a stream or ascends like a stairway into the clouds of a heavenly sky. There is also the representation of the deceased pet crossing the bridge and being joined by many other animals from nature. All animals are so happy to be with each other. It is a very inspiring scene, and artists and writers generally convey a sense of joy and peacefulness in the pet's life in heaven. Online verses are sometimes published as messages from the spirit of the pet to the owner, telling them not to be sad. There is always an optimistic message at the end, assuring they will once again be rejoined.

There were many life-and-death lessons that emerged within the touching narrative of Brighton's final journey. It seemed like an inspired litany of Brighton's B-RIGHT-ON lessons about life, woven into a tapestry of wisdom about sadness and legacy.

1. **Life span**

Life span is reality. The life span numbers for various pets have been established from scientific research and evidence. When the life expectancy of a pet is published, the higher boundary is reality in terms of expected years before death. Anything beyond that number is a grace, blessing, bonus, dessert, or luck. In most cases for dogs, the number thirteen falls in that *bonus* blessing, and beyond thirteen is extraordinary. Brighton lived until the age of thirteen years, five months, which was truly a grace.

2. **Unconditional love**

The pure love of a dog is an experience in unconditional love. The animal communicator explained that Brighton had been a living experience in divine love.

3. Faith

The traditional sequence in religious quotations has been faith, hope, and love. Yet Brighton's gradual passing seemed like a testament to faith becoming the reality that transcends hope. When hope is gone, we rely on faith and love to sustain us.

4. God and dog

There is a saying that God spelled backwards is dog, or dog spelled in reverse is God. The loving relationship with Brighton was truly a closer connection to the spirit of God and dog.

5. B-RIGHT-ON

"Brighton" was the perfect name, as he truly "Brighton'd" the lives of everyone he met. Plus, as explained in his life story, *Brighton Morning,* he lived lessons of wisdom and guidance to "B-RIGHT-ON!"

6. The Brighton touch

The death of Brighton was profound and devastating. Humans frequently have a closer daily relationship with a dog than with another human being. The bond with Brighton was such a constant connection. The intimacy of physical touch between dog and human is constantly woven into a high-level reciprocal nurturing and love.

7. **Heart dog**

One often feels a particular dog is a heart dog or soul dog, as it connects so completely with one's heart or soul. Brighton was truly my heart dog, connected to my heart forever.

8. **Happy, happy**

As a typical golden retriever, Brighton had such a happy dynamic. He would still want me to be happy after it was his time to transition. He would not want to look down at me and see the end of his life leaving me in constant sadness and grief.

9. **Heartbreak**

Brighton's loss was truly an experience in heartbreak. I have learned that when you get a dog, you sign up for a broken heart. However, it is worth every minute of his or her life.

10. **Mortality**

The loss of Brighton brought to immediate experience the profound and personal experience of mortality. It is a B-RIGHT-ON lesson that death is a reality in the life of every living thing.

11. Palliative care

Eventually there comes a point where medical procedures to prolong a life are questionable or could be more painful than a peaceful passage. We gave Brighton time and care for a peaceful process of impending death, through a palliative, hospice-care decision. In choosing between two gut-wrenching alternatives, it became the B-RIGHT-ON thing to do for Brighton.

12. Present moment

When days were numbered in uncertainty, Brighton taught us the profound lesson of living in the present moment and savoring each second we had with him.

13. Euthanasia

There is a point in age, injury, or illness when a dog is never able to recover, and suffering is the current situation preceding an inevitable death. Brighton gave us signals that his time had come, and, out of love for him, we needed to spare him from further suffering. It was through the unselfish honoring of his spirit that we lovingly gave Brighton permission to leave. In our heartbreaking gesture of devotion, we provided preparation and assistance for his final goodbye, to help him peacefully transition over the rainbow bridge.

14. **Doggone dignity**

In the final months of his life, Brighton lost some basic physical capabilities. It was hard for him to maintain his vibrant demeanor when he could no longer hear, and elimination issues became challenging. We saw firsthand his basic need for the gift of dignity. Life functions eventually eroded in the approach of death, and the respect for dignity became a meaningful factor for consideration.

15. **Grief**

Brighton's loss was a firsthand experience that grief is a painful-yet-normal part of the death of a pet. The grief can be equal to or more than the loss of a human, as the connection is so constant and close. The depth of the grief seems to be as profound as the love experienced in life.

16. **Canine compassion**

The passion felt for Brighton is almost impossible for others to understand unless they have personally loved and lost a beloved canine companion.

17. **Dogs grieve**

Snowdon showed us in the loss of both Brighton and Pops that a dog can also experience grief in losing members of their family.

18. Rainbow bridge

"The rainbow bridge" poem creates a comforting metaphor of the vision of death as crossing a bridge. It is truly a B-RIGHT-ON image that gives comfort and inspires anyone who has lost a pet.

19. Afterlife

The loss of Brighton forced us to ponder the real possibility of afterlife. It was possible for us to see coincidences as signs that could be interpreted as possible messages from Brighton. It also allows for a belief in one day being reunited.

20. Spirit

No one knows for sure if there is an afterlife or spirit. Yet through Brighton I felt the profound experience of witnessing and holding a beloved family member in death. It seemed to affirm the feeling that life somehow leaves the body, yet the spirit energy of that life must transcend into the invisible atmosphere. There is a sense of affirmation of the quote that "Energy cannot be created or destroyed."

The Art of Racing in the Rain

I went through many of my books to prepare a helpful bibliography for this book. The most important book to be on this list was *The Art of Racing in the Rain* (Bright White Light, 2008) by Garth Stein, which was the story and basis of the name Enzo.

How ironic that bright white light would also seem to connect with Brighton!

I pulled my copy of *The Art of Racing in the Rain* off the bookshelf. When I opened it, a profound and synchronistic message jumped out at me! Throughout our life together, Pops would always give me books as gifts, and he had a tradition of inscribing the book with a short message and date. My copy of *The Art of Racing in the Rain* had the following message handwritten on the first page:

"Kathy!
We can learn from Brighton—Merry Xmas
Love, Floyd 12-25-2010.

This was truly a profound B-RIGHT-ON prophesy from Pops and a message that Angel Brighton is part of my life forever—and Angel Pops too!

SONG INSPIRATION

"When It's Love" (by Van Halen)

There was a time in the 1980s when a hit song called "When It's Love" was being played all the time on the radio. During that period, I had been driving on a two-day trip with my son. He loved listening to Van Halen, and the cassette tape in the car played the Van Halen hits for hundreds of miles across America. One song that was a top Van Halen hit was "When It's Love." That song played over and over and registered a permanent spot in my motherly memory bank in connection with my son. In fact, it was the song for the first dance at my son and daughter-in-law's wedding.

"When It's Love" has the message of being able to know it is love, as it lasts forever. That same connection stays with me in the memory of Pops and Brighton. Every time I hear that song, it makes my heart beat faster! It is a hard, pounding rock song, yet as romantic as a soft, passionate love long. If you play it and let the beat parallel the pounding rhythm of your heart, you can feel what I feel in the love of Brighton and Pops forever!

Good Boy, Brighton!

Netherlands pup,
Always the "Good Boy."
Cheering us up.
Pure golden joy.

Young pup, so sweet,
Always on the go.
Friends along the street.
Delighting all he'd know.

Brighton everywhere.
In stores, we shopped.
Loved doggie daycare.
B-RIGHT-ON never stopped.

Years brought surgery.
Star patient of vet.
Doc would worry,
Best boy yet!

Snowdon as brother,
Punky and pest.
Buddy like no other.
B-RIGHT-ON best!

Thirteen years.
To angel above.
The B-RIGHT-ON way.
"Good boy,"
Divine love!

13

....

Angel Acknowledgements

In *Brighton Morning*, there is a chapter on stranger angels. It identifies everyday people who are acting as angels in helping Brighton in his life. Likewise, there were several profound experiences in this book when I felt touched by angel grace in terms of connecting with my story of Brighton's final journey.

Throughout the course of three months, there were significant everyday angels who truly became a blessing of help and understanding. These angels had also experienced the tragic loss of a cherished dog and showed genuine empathy in profound sadness. Their stories have been integrated within some chapters. However, this final chapter is a special acknowledgement of the fur angels and their owners who Brighton'd the rainbow bridge journey and the circuit of love. It also honors the recognition of angel grace that permeates our everyday world. It is ironic that this last chapter bears the frequent rainbow number thirteen.

The complete *Brighton Mourning* story has an extremely sad ending with the deaths of Brighton and Pops. Yet, it is important for me in my loss to close the book with a positive inspiration of spirit in the sense of afterlife. I therefore acknowledge the grace I have actually experienced in everyday people, who are angels among us.

Chapter 1—Dry Eyes
Angel Shilo

When we first decided to bring a golden retriever into our life, Pops had a friend in Canada who was an angel of help to us in our decision and planning. We traveled to Toronto and met Angel Shilo, their beautiful golden retriever. Shilo was six at the time when Brighton arrived. He lived in amazingly good health until the age of fifteen. We were heartbroken when he passed over the rainbow bridge, and I wrote this poem to honor his legacy.

Shilo
by Kathleen Stone

Golden coat, golden heart, our golden boy.
Man's best friend, pure gold, pure joy!
Shilo's gold graced us 'til fifteen years old.
His gold dust story will always be told.
He came to us a darling pup, so new,
With every second, our bond with him grew.
Shilo loved his toys, would squeak every duck.
Each day of his life was pure golden luck.
Shilo's golden coat matched leaves in the fall.
He'd retrieve and romp at every recall.
Winter would ignite Shilo's outdoor fun,
Through ice and snow, he would dive and run.
Our golden loss brings 24-karat tears.
Shilo's gold dusts our memories with priceless years.

Angel Daytona

Pops experienced the loss of a dear childhood friend and remained close with his wife and two children. They welcomed a golden retriever puppy named Daytona that we came to know well. We shared our friends' loss as their special golden sadly passed from cancer at a younger age. Being without a family dog was quite a void, and Daytona's mom decided to rescue a vibrant mixed-breed boy named Jackson. When Angel Jackson died several years later, Jackson's mom waited but then welcomed an English bull dog puppy named Emma. Our friend has been there for us with deep understanding and mutual compassion in our loss of Brighton, and then shared the additional loss of her husband's lifelong friend, Pops. She has inspired me with faith in welcoming a new canine angel, when the rainbow bridge brings another time of inevitable loss.

Chapter 2—Side by Side
Angel Max

Angel Max was a striking golden-haired retriever who crossed the rainbow bridge at the age of thirteen. It was clear that Max had truly been a heart dog, and after five years, his mom was finally able to consider a puppy. Angel Max's mom had been regularly visiting my neighbor and would admire Brighton and Snowdon, asking my advice about getting an English crème golden retriever puppy. I helped her through the process of getting her pup, Scout, who is now Enzo's best "friendo."

Chapter 3—Present Moment
Angel Benson and Angel Katie

We frequently walked Brighton around our village center, becoming golden retriever friends with Angel Benson. Benson's mom and dad eventually welcomed an English crème golden retriever named, of all things, Angel! When Snowdon came along, he developed a passionate love for Angel Benson's mom. Three years before Brighton passed, Angel Benson developed a condition requiring surgery at the age of twelve, and Benson's successful recovery truly made him an inspiring hero. Two years later, Benson's mom sadly recognized that his time had come to cross the rainbow bridge. I was there to listen, honor, and support Angel Benson's mom in that time of loss. Her sweet angel, Benson, like Brighton, would be referred to as her "heart dog." I have read in afterlife books that often there is one dog that is deeply bonded to the heart of its owner.

Their other English crème golden named Angel was showing obvious signs of loss and mourning, and after several months, they rescued another golden retriever named Katie, who crossed the rainbow bridge during the writing of this book.

When Brighton received his diagnosis, I received such support from our Angel Benson friends. They would stop over to visit both Brighton and Snowdon. I could see in their eyes that they recognized in Brighton the similar fading that they had experienced near the end with Benson. Angel Benson's mom knew even more intuitively than I did when it was Brighton's time and felt I was perhaps trying to extend the time before euthanasia a little too long.

When Brighton passed during the night, I texted Angel Benson's mom with a short message saying I was stunned that Brighton was gone. She gave me a compassionate and supportive phone call very early that morning to help me emotionally deal with the immediate situation following Brighton's death. She was truly an angel sent to comfort me and was also the most understanding person in sharing the loss of Pops.

Wisdom of Angel Benson's Mom

Angel Benson's mom had quite a positive influence with her wisdom and deep friendship within Brighton's story. Her support is woven into the tapestry of the whole journey. As I put closure to the full circle of Brighton's story, I have a need to acknowledge that my perspective tends to be somewhat mystical. I am sure my perception may seem illusionary and wrapped in creative interpretation. I admit I am more of a poet than a scientist. Therefore, I go beyond into spiritual meaning that warps a sense of rational and pragmatic interpretation and response. I truly acknowledge that I may be too emotional and otherworldly for many.

I have asked Angel Benson's mom to write a reflection of her wise perception as she watched Pops and me during Brighton's final journey. She has extensive experience with dogs and has supported golden retrievers for years through dog-therapy work and the Good As Gold Golden Retriever Rescue. Her level of dog wisdom is woven into a commonsense pragmatism that far outshines my own. I am deeply blessed with the friendship of Angel Benson's mom, and Snowdon just adores her. What an endorsement! She has written this honest reflection that I feel brings a valuable perspective for the reader of this book.

Final Reflections—Angel Benson's Mom

When Brighton was diagnosed with the splenic tumor, I was fairly sure that it was a hemangiosarcoma, as I had a golden who died with that diagnosis. I know that there was no going back from it—chemo does not work—and it's just a matter of time for the dog. And since Brighton had been failing over the last few months before the diagnosis, I knew that this would end his life. I have always had at least one dog for my entire life, so I "know" when things are coming to an end for my dogs, and I also "know" when it's the last day and time to bring their life to a conclusion. For Brighton, I just wanted Kathy and Floyd to enjoy what time they had with him and to end Brighton's life when it became clear that the end was imminent. That is what we did with the golden we had who died of hemangiosarcoma of the heart. She collapsed one day, and the diagnosis was made that it was most likely this tumor, although I did not have a biopsy. But all signs pointed to it as it did for Brighton. The specialty vet that diagnosed my golden said she could live an hour or even up to a year before the tumor burst. She lived seven happy months. When she collapsed again and was showing signs of blood loss, we had her put down within hours.

But with Kathy and Floyd not having experience with the end of a dog's life—and especially with a soul dog like Brighton, I knew that they would have to research all options—and that's Kathy's way! For the days that they agonized over having the surgery, I wanted to scream, "Absolutely *not*—don't do it!" But I wouldn't, because everyone must do what they have to do. I was thrilled, however, when they decided against surgery.

It was agonizing for me to watch Brighton's decline and Floyd and Kathy's distress and sadness over the last several weeks of Brighton's life. I had hoped that Kathy would put Brighton down when he was experiencing the bad diarrhea and became so weak because I knew that he would only decline and that it would be best for Kathy and Floyd and the dogs to end Brighton's life. From my own experience, having put several dogs to sleep, even with my "soul dog," Benson, there was a great relief to see their suffering over. We were always sad, especially with Benson, but there was a calm that came over me after it was over because I knew that I had made the right decision and that they had transferred to a different place where they were young and whole and running around like they used to. There was sadness, but it was a "sweet sadness" for me. I saw them happy in my mind's eye.

Again, though, it was Kathy's decision and not mine, so I had to support her in whatever she did, and I think I accomplished that. After Brighton died, and because Kathy had done what she felt was best for her family at the end of Brighton's life, I thought that she would experience some of the same "sweet sadness" of a wonderful life concluded. My biggest surprise in all of this is that she did not. She was very, very grief stricken for a long period of time. Having a spiritual nature, I thought that she would connect to Brighton in his new place in somewhat of the same way that I had with Benson and that she would be able to see that the gift of his life with her would comfort her. But it did not. And that was surprising for me! However, I think Kathy is doing much better now, and I am very glad that we all got to experience the magic of Brighton!

Angel Princess

Angel Benson's mom had the sad loss of her grandbaby fur angel named Princess. She gave me many details about the beautiful life of Princess, and I wove the details into a memorial poem. Poetry can be a beautiful way to honor a fur angel.

Furry-Tail Princess

A Cinderella story,
a furry-tail life.
Princess, our resident angel,
In good times and in strife.

The pal of our grizzled ole neighbor,
Mr. Ed did best to care.
Guarding dog protects failing master,
Nursing home visits to share.

Princess would push against the fence,
to seek an endearing scratch.
We soon learned that this lady's love,
could never find a match.

An enchanted Sherwood Forest,
her backyard was Princess's place.
Loved chasing squirrels and chipmunks,
Justin's look of amazing grace!

She once jumped off the high back deck,
Ate anything near and far.
Stole and ate a chicken bone
that sent her to ER.

She passed a test of tenacity
and also passed that bone.
Grand prize, an ingested knee sock,
proudly exiting it alone!
Truly a lady-in-waiting,
Princess's passion for each knight.

At bedtime would do her "perimeter check"
So everything was all right.

Finally, with blanket she would cuddle,
alongside Becky's bed.
Beneath mattress and curtain,
she'd veil her velvet, soft head.

She liked to be with everyone,
choosing closet in a storm.
Snuggling by bed and bathroom door,
her ritual each morn.

Princess, our Lady Lambie,
crowning glory with each groom.
Winking to us with unique ears,
One proudly standing, one bowed down.

A black ring was her signet,
circling furry tail so fine.
Honey-colored coat, her breed mix,
surely hard to define.

White-tipped paws, always crossed,
Her ladylike delicate gloves.
Glowing mask brightened her face,
a blessing from above.

Forever an angel halo,
that crowns her love so loyal.
Our lopsided ear,
Furry-tail Princess,
Heart of gold…
forever royal!

Chapter 4—Hope, Faith, Love
Angels Aries and Rocco

In the journey through the three hospice months, I will always remember the frequent contacts from my dear friend, who was the mom of Angel Aries and two Angels named Rocco. In earlier family life, my angel friend had a beloved husky dog named Aries, who they had lost in his older age. Then they tragically had their flat-coat retriever, Rocco, die at age three from a tumor on his spine. Subsequently, they had a second Rocco die at age eight from overvaccination. I will never forget how traumatized I felt for Angel Rocco's mom and dad at the double heartbreak of losing of both Angel Rocco flat-coat retrievers. Due to their tragedy, I was left forever with tremendous anxiety every time I had my dogs scheduled for a regular vaccination.

As you can only imagine, my dear angel friend was able to empathize with me through her own experiences with the loss of her three precious angels. She had such a deep compassion I could feel every time I related my update on Brighton's gradual-yet-peaceful decline. She was also a dear friend to Pops and would often send him emails of support and encouragement with understanding friendship. I feel this frequent support was truly the touch of an angel. Plus, my angel friend's name is Angie!

Angel Hershey

One special angel was part of my school's office staff, and we had a special dog-lover bond between her dachshunds and my golden retrievers. Her older dachshund named Hershey was aging gracefully. In his teen years, Hershey made the heartbreaking journey over the rainbow bridge. I wrote a very special poem in memory of Angel Hershey's life.

The Hersh

The Hersh, a cherished lap dog quilt.
Patchwork'd his sweet chocolate life.
Legacy of a good boy lovingly built,
Years of Hershey kissed joy and strife.
As a weiner hot dog at Halloween,
Wore mustard, ketchup, squeezed in bun.
Antlers or Santa Hat for the Christmas scene,
His darling dachshund stocking number one!

Hersh, a Packer fan through and through,
With green and gold jersey dressed up.
Packer collar and leash, we all knew.
He was a diehard Green Bay weiner pup!
Waiting patiently at the bedroom door,
Time ticked for Tim's wake each morn.
Nosing newspaper to see our faces even more
Nudging the bowl for beloved popcorn.

Hersh adored Vegas stays with Holly.
Lily's love of this little sun god.
He'd high-five and spin 'round so jolly!
Weiner rollovers on command with his bod.
Amy's snuggling and soft pet before school.
Hip surgery, three weeks of nights, Pam's chair.
If sick, never leaving your side was the rule.
The doggie nurse of family love and care.
Hersh was a therapy dog of rare kind.

Gram's baby in rehab, patiently fun.
No leash, he'd never leave the room,
Then strut the hall, charming everyone.
Hersh waited for treats after business outside.
After bath, such a handsome parade!
His soft, thin ears always clean with pride.
Tim's "little man" bank trips ... treats paid!

Hersh would "go to Sissy" with excited barks.
Quieting his woofs with, "Hersh, it's me!"
He grew to fear thunder and fireworks,
Yet a twelve-pound *big dog* personality!
A little trooper through and through,
Crampy leg, bruises, bumps, our fear.
Massaging sprained neck,
Off the deck he once flew,
Screeching car, aches and scratches, oh dear!

When Hersh was nine, Hazel arrived.
She'd love him each night with her snuggle.
Sharing their *Weiners* bowl he did survive.
With his last day, Hazel ... a dazed struggle.
Hersh's litter of five, Dad Harley, Mom Molly,
Born December 26, 1999.
A Santa pup for Pam, Tim, Amy, and Holly
Sweet sixteen birthday plans left behind.

Hershey's last day was a Packer Sunday passage.
We never left his side in final sleep.
A *good, good boy*, our last message.
Our October 19, heartbreak so deep.
Run fast, little big man, to Grams, run fast.
You seemed lost in time when she'd gone.
Her big Hershey kiss,
"Over the Rainbow" will last.
As your sweet, sweet Hershey kiss lives on.

Chapter 5—Good Boy, Goodbye
Angel Heroes Gold

English crème golden retrievers were less well known in the United States when I acquired Brighton. I gradually became acquainted with a breeder, and our mutual passion for the English crème golden retriever developed into an ongoing deep friendship. The breeder's older dogs were golden heroes similar in age to Brighton. Heroes Gold's mom is so extremely thorough in investigating pedigree and health data that I affectionately call her Sherlock.

Sherlock also is a valued member of the staff of a veterinary clinic and has extremely compassionate experience with the rainbow bridge passage of her own hero angels as well as those from the clinic. Sherlock was by my side as a friend and angel from the time of Brighton's tumor diagnosis, through hospice, and helping find a wonderful at-home vet. When Brighton passed in the middle of the night, Sherlock was one of the first angels I texted for comfort. Early that morning, she became my angel hero, listening and guiding me through the painful steps that immediately followed sudden death.

Sherlock provided significant advice guiding me to acquire Snowdon and Enzo. She had also been a facilitator of two breeding opportunities for Snowdon to father pups, which became a comforting legacy of Brighton and Snowdon's pedigree lineage from the Netherlands.

Chapter 6—Phoenix Arising
Angel Chief

It was always exciting to find any English crème goldens in the United States that had come from Brighton's breeder in the Netherlands. In Indiana, I found a pup named Maui who was a nephew of Snowdon. Maui's mom had the heartbreaking loss of her golden retriever named Chief the year before. Angel Chief had been a very similar age to Brighton, and Angel Chief's mom gave me all the details she could about her experience with hemangiosarcoma, in-home euthanasia, and cremation. This was priceless angel advice in helping me through all decisions related to Brighton's cancer, death, and cremation.

Chapter 7—Rainbow Dots
Angel Max

Through Facebook, there appeared a true surprise angel in someone with a unique gift of almost being like my twin in cyberspace. In fact, we call each other "twinship." My twinship especially identified with my loss of Brighton, as it was like the loss of her heart golden named Max. She would tell me about Max and his eventual passing in an effort to affirm all the beautiful things I had done for Brighton. Her experience with the death of her heart dog had so many parallels of anguish with my own loss. Max had died several years earlier, and, after Max, she had two other dogs who tragically passed before she acquired her current three goldens.

After losing her dogs, Twinship had connected with a highly

reputable holistic veterinarian. She was able to secure the name of a well-known animal communicator who had appeared on television and radio who connected with animals in the afterlife. I immediately followed up on her excellent reputation, and, by phone, arranged a session for the animal communicator to connect me with Brighton.

Our mutual animal communicator experience took our Twinship into the realm of sharing deeper understanding about the afterlife. I asked her in all seriousness one day if she would try to contact Brighton for me. As a result she was able to share a report of her experience in a beautiful light-filled apparition of Brighton. He was happy to connect with her and convey his message to her of his forever love connection with me. Twinship was literally overwhelmed with a feeling of grace in genuinely believing she had seen and heard from Brighton. Since that day, Brighton is our spirit angel that we share. We often see synchronistic signs that can be perceived as a message from my boy.

Chapter 8—Adios, Yet Not Goodbye
Angel Lourdes and Angel Nielson

I learned to see breeders as angels that bring such forever love to so many families. Brighton was born at the Morning Valley Kennel in the Netherlands. Brighton's mother was Angel Lourdes, who was named after the Shrine of the Blessed Mother in France. Brighton's father was Angel Nielson, whose registered name was Dream Max an Apple a Day. Brighton's rich heritage was the foundation for his Yoda spirit throughout his life.

Chapter 9—Circuit of Bright
<u>Angel Ans</u>

Angel Ans of the Morning Valley has truly been an angel to me from the time she first honored us with a pup from the litter of Angel Lourdes. That had been over thirteen years earlier, when Brighton was born, and then again six years later with Snowdon. Now, I was again feeling her grace as we communicated about the litter conceived the Easter Monday after Brighton had died and that was due to be born in June. This litter would have all the heritage going back to Brighton's parents, Angels Lourdes and Nielson, and would produce our new pup, Taste of Lemon of the Morning Valley, Enzo!

The connection with our cherished breeder in the Netherlands has been truly a special dynamic in my life. Over the years, since I received Brighton, I have tried to find others in the United States with English crème golden retrievers from the same breeder. There is one English crème golden breeder a couple hundred miles from me who also has a male from Brighton's Netherlands breeder, and we keep in contact as a kind of mutual Morning Valley admiration society. I have also been in touch with a brother of Snowdon who lives out East, as well as another breeder in the East who has English crème golden retrievers with the Morning Valley pedigree.

Chapter 10—S.O.S.
<u>Angel James and Angel Michelle</u>

Pops and our son, James, were the best of friends, and their sudden, unexpected parting was sad beyond words. James and his angel wife, Michelle, immediately flew from their home in Texas and were truly both angels who literally landed and surrounded me with wings of comfort. They were with me every moment of this S.O.S. tragedy, with grace in orchestrating all the funeral arrangements and sharing profound grief.

Chapter 11—"It's Me"
Angel Pops

Chapter 11 is devoted to honoring the loving memory of our beloved angel Pops. Pops had been my silent angel, being there for me through the whole journey of Brighton's passing. Then he shared the grief that permeated our home with Brighton's loss in December and then the quarantine of COVID-19 coming soon after in February. During the COVID quarantine time, I was writing this book, and Pops was dealing with increased heart issues. Metaphorically, it seemed our home was the house of broken hearts. By summer, the original manuscript was complete, and Pops had begun doing the initial reading of the draft and shared his comments. Ironically, Pops had only finished chapter 4 when Enzo arrived and completely disrupted the COVID quarantine quiet with his puppy barks! Three weeks after Enzo arrived, Pops suddenly received his own angel call to join Brighton as my two forever angels.

Chapter 12—B-RIGHT-ON
Angel Brighton

Brighton has been the lead angel in this whole story of his life and beyond that is meant to B-RIGHT-ON. It is hoped he will "Brighton" the life of everyone who reads his story.

Chapter 13—Angel Acknowledgements
School Angels

There were times when one of several teacher friends had a dog who passed over the rainbow bridge. Teachers are members of a very caring profession and inherently manifest the gift of compassion and outreach for those experiencing grief in pet loss.

Angels Missy and Louise

I came to truly be enchanted with the husky breed through a passionate dog-lover teacher friend. The first husky I knew was Angel Missy, a beautiful rescue. Brighton was still well when twelve-year-old Missy suddenly crossed the rainbow bridge a few weeks before Christmas. Feeling very sad for Missy's loss, I found a perfect Secret Santa remembrance to have delivered to Missy's mom. It was a life-size plush animal husky dog, and I had it looking festive with a doggie Christmas scarf tied around the husky's neck. The Secret-Santa surprise brought a tearful message of understanding, which is sometimes all we can do to console someone who has lost a cherished family fur angel. A picture of the husky at the front window became a Facebook "howl-i-day" posting to honor Angel Missy.

What was amazing is that the husky story continued to howl on. With the snows of winter, Angel Missy's mom continued to check out her familiar husky rescue group. There were a pair of husky sisters available for adoption, but they could not be separated. They had the cutest names of Thelma and Louise, and at that time were involved in dogsled racing. Angel Missy's mom began attending the snowy winter events and getting to know Thelma and Louise and their foster family. Eventually, a month later, Thelma and Louise were adopted and came to multiply the howling that had been absent in Angel Missy's home.

Several months after the arrival of Thelma and Louise, it was discovered that Louise had terminal cancer, and within a few months joined Angel Missy over the rainbow bridge. Again, it was sad husky howling, yet Angels Missy and Louise then sent Husky Kira to bring new joy to grieving Thelma and her family. The life-size toy husky now oversees the guest bedroom from the top bunk of the bunk beds because Kira loves toys and would playfully chew it to shreds. This is such a beautiful story of dog rescue that shows what is often a circuit of grace that brings new joy to this side of the rainbow bridge.

Angels Emma and Abigail Rose, Good girl

Another school friend lost her black lab, Emma, who sadly crossed the rainbow bridge, followed by Abby. When Abby passed, I was able to find a life-size plush black lab and write a poem in her honor. During the writing of this book, Angel Abby's mom has acquired another black lab puppy named Martha.

Abby Rose, Good Girl

Forever memories cherish Emma and Abby…
Always there making happy from crabby.

Now playing together in rainbow paradise.
Sending love to you… in plush disguise.

Precious touch of angels, impossible to replace,
Constant reminders will never erase.

Bless Abby and Emma in heaven above.
Their spirits always with you in
Huge hugs of God's love!

256

Facebook Angels

Brighton had passed over the rainbow bridge in December. In January, I continued to remain part of the rainbow bridge and canine cancer groups. In my own grief, I now had such an outpouring of empathy toward others and followed a calling to reach out to others in a canine compassion ministry. I was positively connecting with others on Facebook every day. For some, I would console others in loss, while many times, I would show golden retrievers, puppies, and delightful videos intended to "Brighton" the lives of others, with the continuing theme of "B-RIGHT-ON."

Angel Paddy Corrigan

There was a special golden retriever Facebook page I had been following every day for over a year. The page hosted amazing daily videos of a curly coated English golden retriever named Paddy and his life with his dad, Tony Corrigan, in the beautiful English countryside of Leeds, United Kingdom.

On a Thursday in early July, there was a tragic post that Paddy was being taken to the vet and was showing signs of a possible stroke. Hundreds of Paddy's fans in many countries were very worried and sent thoughts and prayers to his owner. By Saturday, there was a GoFundMe page set up by one of many devoted followers in Washington, DC. By Sunday, ten thousand dollars had been donated to help support Paddy's treatment and recovery.

Like everyone else, I was extremely fond of Paddy's daily video journeys, with one picture more beautiful than the next. I felt the anxiety of a severe golden retriever illness and the threat of death that haunts all of us. As weeks and months moved along, Paddy received medications, physical therapy, and the most loving care possible from his owner. Paddy made a miraculous recovery, which gave us renewed faith that death is not always the imminent outcome of serious fur angel maladies. Two months later, Brighton received his tumor diagnosis. I continued to follow Paddy every day during Brighton's end-of-life journey and beyond. There was true inspiration and joy in Paddy's story of recovery and continued resilience. It was during the final stages of this book that Paddy crossed the rainbow bridge and was mourned by hundreds around the world and, most certainly, by me.

Tony courageously continued to keep Paddy alive in spirit for us as he posted daily pictures and videos, sharing his deep grief at Paddy's loss. Two months later, Tony's Facebook followers were able to celebrate with him the arrival of a new golden retriever puppy named Murphy, who carries part of the pedigree of Angel Paddy.

Angel Owen

I had been following Facebook posts from an English crème golden retriever breeder in the southeastern part of France. While attending a Paris dog show, one dog had become hospitalized. Two other dogs waited with the breeder in Paris until this dog could be released. Soon after returning home, the breeder had a second tragic situation of several of her pups becoming ill from a vaccine reaction, and one precious pup, Angel Owen, sadly died while the others needed careful attention to slowly recover. My intense concern for the loss of Angel Owen led to a long-distance Facebook friendship, where I continue to celebrate the joys of her dogs and puppies that shine her way.

Shine Your Way, Owen

Jimmy and Joy on July 11
Seven little wonders sent from heaven.
Three males, four females, one cuter than other.
A special angel as the little brother.

Mr. Vert, Mr. Bleu, Mr. Turquoise,
Three precious little boys
Miss Rouge, Miss Verte, Miss Jaune, Miss Rose,
Four gorgeous girls, heaven knows!

All pups loved as a perfect pup.
Twelve weeks of miraculous growing up!
One little prince especially known.
The beautiful angel boy named Owen.

Pictures of pups all Facebook attention.
Each video too priceless to mention.
Owen would somehow especially shine.
Never knowing, not meant to be mine.

Puppies growing fast, July to October.
Would never expect Owen's life to be over.
October 13, his sweet life suddenly gone.
Rainbow bridge to become his forever home.

Devastated at little Owen's passing.
Pain of his loss, a void everlasting.
Sad words from hundreds on Facebook unfurled.
Legacy of Angel Owen spread thru the world.

Passion Breeding in Shine Your Way.
Heaven in Provence, Owen forever to stay.
Yet Owen's angel life lives on in spirit.
Bark of his joy, we'll always hear it!

259

<u>Angel Kayleigh</u>

Another Facebook angel appeared in conjunction with Brighton's thirteenth birthday on July 4. Brighton received a birthday greeting from a female golden who would also be celebrating her thirteenth birthday during the following two weeks. Through Facebook, we had Brighton develop a Valentine-type friendship with his female age mate. Kayleigh celebrated her birthday, and a few days later, she was taken to the vet and diagnosed with a tumor on her liver that was inoperable due to her age.

Brighton's health was fine at the time of Kayleigh's diagnosis, and we began having Brighton post Facebook messages of love and support. By late August, Kayleigh's situation was under control with meds but with uncertainty as to the amount of time she had left. My heartfelt caring and support continued to be extended, not knowing that by September 5, Brighton would be diagnosed with a tumor of the spleen and given three months to live. During Brighton's final months, his golden girlfriend continued to do quite well. We rejoice at the Facebook photos of Kayleigh's stable and happy life and continue to celebrate her story far beyond Brighton's passing.

It was quite ironic that Kayleigh was diagnosed with her tumor first and yet Brighton passed more quickly. At the time of this writing, they celebrated Kayleigh's vitality and fifteenth birthday! However, just before the holidays, Kayleigh also crossed the rainbow bridge to join Brighton. Shortly after the past new year, Kayleigh's family honored her precious golden retriever legacy by welcoming a male puppy who was named Luke, after Luke Skywalker. Kayleigh's family has such a deep golden-retriever passion that welcoming a golden retriever puppy is their way of healing the profound void of Kayleigh's loss and honoring her legacy with the legacy of angelic golden retriever spirit returning to their home. Kayleigh has sent rainbow dots to her family, which they see as signs from her that she is happy to see them recover, while she knows their golden girl will never be replaced or forgotten by the arrival of a romping little boy pup!

Angel Fahrenheit (Theo)

As described in chapter 2, during the month of Brighton's thirteenth birthday, I became aware of a Morning Valley pup that had unexpectedly become available. An English crème golden retriever breeder in Arkansas was picking up the pup named Fahrenheit and invited me to join her in welcoming the pup shipped from the Netherlands to Chicago. I continue to maintain a caring interest in this pup that now has the beautiful name Theo.

Angel Harley

Bella and Harley were littermates, and through a tragic circumstance, Angel Harley crossed over the rainbow bridge unexpectedly. Bella was totally heartbroken, and I read with empathic sadness the Facebook crisis that Bella's mom was having with her anguish at the loss of Harley. A few months after Angel Harley's passing, Bella's grief was lifted by the surprise of a new puppy named Benny. Bella and Benny have since had a litter of puppies! The story of Angel Harley was a sign for me that happiness can follow the mourning of the tragic loss of a fur angel. Benny could not be a replacement for Angel Harley but rather was an additional joy bringing the resurrection in afterlife spirit!

Angels Cobe and Callie Rose

Angel Cobe's pack live in Green Bay and, of course, are Green Bay Packer fans! What would be the chances that my native Chicago husband was also an avid Packer Backer his whole life? The Packer connection grew during the fall when Brighton was in hospice, and Cobe's pack adorned Facebook photos with delightful green and gold football garb. When Brighton passed, Cobe's mom posted messages on Facebook that permeated my soul with such genuine compassion.

In early February, Angel Cobe was diagnosed with an unexpected medical condition that tragically took his life in a much shorter timespan than Brighton. It was my turn to try to provide comfort to a dear friend in one of those situations where loss is totally unexpected. I ordered a crystal dog to send to Angel Cobe's mom, with the hope that she might also find some comfort in rainbow dots sent to her from Angel Cobe. It is amazing how my year of challenge and loss had come full circle. Yet, the loss of Angel Cobe launched a year of many difficult challenges for Cobe's mom. Through our shared grief, we developed a rainbow bridge friendship, guided by Angel Cobe and Angel Brighton, who were recently joined by Cobe's sister, Angel Callie Rose, who sadly passed during the writing of this book.

Angels Over the Rainbow

In the year prior to Brighton's thirteenth birthday, I had become very involved with several golden retriever and English crème golden retriever Facebook groups. One very meaningful group was

Somewhere Over the Rainbow Pet Loss Remembrance and Support. There were numerous posts every day, and some would convey very sad news of a fur angel passing over the rainbow bridge, leaving such tragic messages that would break my heart. I knew the saying, "There but for the grace of God, go I." Sooner or later, I knew Brighton's life would fade into transition and the afterlife.

I felt a tremendous compassion in the anguish of the rainbow bridge posts. Although I was not yet dealing with the personal loss of Brighton, my sense of empathy turned into a mission or calling to post condolence comments that would honor the grief of others. Joining this one group led to several other pet grief support groups, and my condolence responses to pet loss have become a daily ministry.

Angels Cecilia and Bridgit

The founder of the "Somewhere Over the Rainbow Pet Loss Remembrance and Support" group is a psychologist located in New Jersey. Her introductory welcome to the group is filled with genuine compassion and understanding of the tremendous grief that is experienced in the loss of a pet. It is also a deep, emotional loss that most who are not pet owners cannot fully understand. Therefore, this Facebook group has been a lifesaver every day for the owners of pets who express the most profound anguish and heartbreak, drowning in tears that will not subside.

The rainbow pet loss group founder experienced personal heartbreak in the loss of her two golden retriever girls, Angel Cecilia and Angel Bridgit. Therefore, she is a deeply personal facilitator of an inspired ministry. She has also published a beautiful book: *And I Love You Still: A Thoughtful Guide and Remembrance Journal for Healing the Loss of a Pet.*

The book does a beautiful job of guiding others through personal journal reflections in the profound path of grief over the loss of their pet. It was truly an Angel connection that brought Angel Cecilia and Angel Bridgit's mom into my life. It was meant to be for me to connect with her compassionate outreach and ministry, as there is a genuine need for support in pet loss and grief.

Angel Emily Snow and Noah

One of the most profound angel stories began when Brighton was only twelve and had just successfully completed his first eye surgery. As part of one golden retriever Facebook group, I had begun to follow a dream-theme English crème golden breeder who had experienced the tragic loss of her two-year-old angel, Emily Snow, to a very rare and debilitating autoimmune disorder. Angel Emily Snow's mom posted on the one-year anniversary of her passing that Emily Snow had "taken a big piece of my heart with her." Emily's dad posted on YouTube the most incredible video describing Emily Snow's puppyhood, unexpected symptoms, and the heroic efforts to identify, treat, and save her life.

There was a joyful Facebook announcement from Angel Emily Snow's mom in August, following Brighton's thirteenth birthday. A new dream litter had been born, and there were three pups in the litter: Moses, Grace, and Noah! During Brighton's hospice, the pups grew, and two were placed in forever homes. One, named Noah, had some difficulties, and I became very involved in helping Emily's mom find the right forever home for a special-needs pup. At six months of age, Noah finally found a special home, and both Emily's mom and Noah's new mom have become dear angel friends.

SONG INSPIRATION

"I'm Your Angel" (by Celine Dion, lyrics by Celine Dion and R. Kelly)

There were several times in my life that I felt alone on a journey of destiny. I had been comforted by the lyrics of the song "I'm Your Angel." Throughout Brighton's journey, there have been everyday angels that Brighton brought into my life.

I have had a lifelong passion for mountains. The song affirms my inspiration for the heavenly metaphor of the mountaintop. I had actually developed a fascination for the Swiss mountain called the Matterhorn. On numerous visits, I gained a sense of the divine in looking up to the Matterhorn, hiking high, and flying above the mountaintop several times in a helicopter. The song's lyrics integrate the concept of morning coming if you believe. It is no coincidence for me to see the symbolic relationship between the words *morning* and *mourning*. The final stanza inspires comfort in the *bright* of the sun. *Brighton Morning* was truly an angelic name for my boy!

The mourning aspect of the song is a reminder that tears are part of life. It also honors profound loss and subsequent aloneness. Yet, there is also faith that paves the way of grief and guidance along the way with an eternal angel spirit. This passage of Angel Brighton has been "Brighton'd" by faith in the afterlife. It inspired me to believe in the message of the refrain that an angel will be present in many forms, and that there are silent messages in songs and words said by others. Finally, there is the encouragement of grace, compassion, courage, and trust until the end and forever.

Yes, I have faith that Brighton is my angel, and he brought angels into my life. Now, Brighton is with Angel Pops. They watch over Snowdon, Enzo, and me, and bless us through a flock of everyday angels that continually bless our lives.

Resources

The author has personally read or reviewed the resources listed and finds support in dealing with the various aspects of pet loss.

Anderson, Karen A. *The Amazing Afterlife of Animals: Messages and Signs from our Pets on the Other Side.* Lexington, KY: Painted Rain Publishing, 2017

Anderson, Karen A. *Hear All Creatures! The Journey of an Animal Communicator.* Woonsocket, RI: New River Press, 2008.

Atwater, Brent. *After Death Signs from Pet Afterlife and Animals in Heaven.* Monee, IL: Just Plain Love Books, 2018.

Bekoff, Marc. *The Emotional Lives of Animals: A Leading Scientist Explores Animal Joy, Sorrow, and Empathy and Why They Matter.* Novato, CA: New World Library, 2007.

Burgess, Brian. *We Will See Our Pets in Heaven: The Afterlife of Animals from a Biblical Perspective.* Outskirts Press, 2013.

Cameron, W. Bruce. *A Dog's Purpose: A Novel for Humans.* Tom Doherty Associates, 2010.

Cooper, Candi Cane. *Afterlife of Animals: A Guide to Healing from Loss and Communicating with Your Beloved Pet.* Emeryville, CA: Rockridge Press, 2020.

Corbin, Julianne C. *And I Love You Still...A Thoughtful Guide and Remembrance Journal for Healing the Loss of a Pet.* Middletown, DE: Julianne C. Corbin Publisher, 2020.

Curtis, Simon (Director). *The Art of Racing in the Rain* [Film]. 20th Century Fox, 2019.

D'Arcy, Paula. *Gift of the Red Bird – The Story of a Divine Encounter.* New York: Crossroad Publishing Company, 1996.

Dodman, Nicholas. *Good Old Dog – Expert Advice for Keeping Your Aging Dog Happy, Healthy, and Comfortable.* Boston, MA: Mariner Books Houghton Mifflin Harcourt, 2010.

Francisco, Wendy. *GoD and DoG.* New York: Hachette Book Group, 2010.

Friedman, Russell, James, Cole, James, John W. *The Grief Recovery Handbook for Pet Loss.* Lanham, MD: Taylor Trade Publishing, 2014.

Greiner, Gregg T. *The Laugh a Minute Clinic.* Aurora, IL: Kelmscott Communications, 2010.

Grogan, John. *Marley & Me - Life and love with the World's Worst Dog.* New York: Harper Collins Publishing, 2005

Frankel, David (Director). *Marley & Me* [Film]. 20th Century Fox., 2008.

Hallstrom, Lasse (Director). *A Dog's Purpose* [Film]. Universal Pictures, 2017.

Hawn, Roxanne. *Heart Dog – Surviving the Loss of Your Canine Soul Mate.* Middletown, DE, 2015

Katz, Jon. *Going Home – Finding Peace When Pets Die.* New York: Random House, 2012.

King, Barbara J. *How Animals Grieve.* Chicago, IL: The University of Chicago Press, 2013.

Koontz, Dean. *A Big Little Life – A Memoir of a Joyful Dog Named Trixie.* Bantam Books, 2009.

Kowalski, Gary. *Goodbye, Friend – Healing Wisdom for Anyone Who Has Ever Lost a Pet.* Novato, CA: New World Library, 2012.

Kurz, Gary. *Wagging Tails in Heaven – The Gift of Our Pets' Everlasting Love.* New York: Citadel Press Books, 2011.

McGahan, Kate. *Jack McAfghan's Return from Rainbow Bridge.* Kate McGahan Publisher: Monee, IL, 2021.

McGahan, Kate. *Jack McAfghan – Reflections on Life with My Master – A Dog's Memoir on Life After Death.* Kate McGahan Publisher: Monee, IL, 2015.

McGahan, Kate. *The Lizard from Rainbow Bridge – A True Tale of an*

Unexpected Angel. Kate McGahan Publisher: Monee, IL, 2021.

McGahan, Kate. *Only Gone from Your Sight – Jack McAfghan's Little Guide to Pet Loss and Grief.* Kate McGahan Publisher: Monee, IL, 2018.

Ragan, Lyn. *Signs from the Afterlife – Identifying Gifts from the Other Side.* Monee, IL: Lyn Ragan Publisher. 2014

Ragan, Lyn. *Signs from Pets in the Afterlife – Identifying Messages from Pets in Heaven.* Lexington, KY: Afterlife Communications, 2015.

Severino, Elizabeth. *The Animals' Viewpoint on Dying, Death, and Euthanasia*. Turnersville, NJ: The Healing Connection, 2002.

Sheridan, Kim. *Animals and the Afterlife – True Stories of Our Best Friends' Journey Beyond Death*. Carlsbad, CA: Hay House Inc, 2003.

Smith, Jacquelin. *Animal Communication – Our Sacred Connection*. Lakeville, MN: Galde Press, 2015.

Smith, Jacquelin. *Star Origins and Wisdom of Animals – Talks With Animal Souls*. Bloomington, IN: AuthorHouse, 2010.

Smith, Penelope. *Animals in Spirit – Our Faithful Companions' Trandition to the Afterlife*. New York: Atria Books, 2008.

Smith, Penelope. *Animal Talk – Interspecies Telepathic Communication*. New York: Atria Books, 2008.

Stein, Garth. *The Art of Racing in the Rain*. New York: Harper Collins Publisher, 2008.

Williams, Marta. *Learning Their Language – Intuitive Communication with Animals and Nature*. Novato, CA: New World Library, 2003.

Wintz, Friar Jack). *I Will See You in Heaven*. Brewster, MA: Paraclete Press, 2018.

Woodward, Steven H. *Biblical Proof Animals Do Go to Heaven*. Maitland, FL: Xulon Press, 2019.

Woodward, Steven H. *BJ: A Dog's Journey into the Afterlife*. Maitland, FL: Xulon Press, 2018

Woodward, Steven H. *God's Revelations of Animals and People.* Maitland, FL: Xulon Press, 2018.

Woodward, Steven H. *How to Recover from the Heartbreak of Pet Loss.* Maitland, FL: Xulon Press, 2019.

Wycherley, Jeannie. *Losing My Best Friend –Thoughtful Support for Those Affected by Dog Bereavement of Pet Loss.* Monee, IL: Bark At the Moon Books, 2018.

SONG REFERENCES

Each of the 13 chapters of **Brighton Mourning** includes a reflection on a particular song that became an inspiration to the author within the circumstances of the memoir. Credit is fully given to the song title and recording artist(s), and the song is recognized and acknowledged for its contribution to the support found in the grief process.

Ch.	Title of Song	Artist(s)
1	Dry Your Eyes	Neil Diamond
2	By My Side	Musical: Godspell
3	Nothin' But A Heartache	Neil Diamond
4	Endless Love	Lionel Richie, Diana Ross
5	See Me, Feel Me	The Who - Musical Tommy
6	I've Been This Way Before	Neil Diamond
7	To Where You Are	Josh Groban
8	Spanish Eyes	Willie Nelson, Julio Iglesias
9	Circle of Life	Elton John
10	Sound of Silence	Simon & Garfunkel
11	Faithfully	Journey
12	When It's Love	Van Halen
13	I'm, Your Angel	Celine Dion, R. Kelly

About the Author

Kathleen Stone has a PhD in Educational Psychology from Loyola University Chicago. Her professional expertise includes over thirty-five years of teaching experience in public education in grades K-8, plus Library/Media, district director of gifted and talented education, and research in comparative and international education. Her previous book is *Brighton Morning —Doggone Wags of Wisdom to B-RIGHT-ON*. It is a chapter book written for children ages eight to eleven and presents a dog's point of view in the life of her golden retriever named Brighton. Kathleen is passionate about her English crème golden retriever named Brighton, Snowdon, and Enzo, all born in the Netherlands. She has always used her expertise in educational psychology to warmly address the socioemotional needs of children and adults. With genuine empathy, she shares a Facebook ministry to support those dealing with heartbreak and grief in pet loss. Kathleen lives in a suburb of Chicago and, since retiring, has been writing inspirational narratives, two poetry books, and maintains her website <u>www.Insteadinternational.com,</u> sharing access to her international conference presentations on Gifted & Talented Education and research in PISA international testing.

Printed in the United States
by Baker & Taylor Publisher Services